The things people say about Gary Courtenay

"I recently used mentors4business.com to launch a business a…
explained what I wanted to do and they wrote the sale…
prospective members. CEO Gary Courtenay … h
and was marked 'excellent' by almost every…
entertaining; he gave truly valuable insights …
could use at once. Importantly he inspired eve…
After the event I told him: "Using mentors4bus…
a box, all we had to do was send out your letters … of
itself." We now have a thriving club with aroun…
I wouldn't hesitate to recommend Gary Court… business.com to
anybody who appreciates a big result with the min… effort."

Dr Philip Hallam, past Professor of University of Central England and now MD of RDI UK, specialists in university accredited distance learning

"I would like to thank you for your excellent contribution throughout the Masterclass on 'How To Build a Better Organisation' at Cranfield University. Your particular session on maximising results from Direct Mail was focussed very well combining humour, principles and practical hands-on operating tips."

Maxwell Selman – Cranfield University Visiting Lecturer

"Unlike many people working in his field Gary doesn't just supply general advice, he offers specific strategies and then does everything he can to help you follow through. His input is challenging and his approach is sensitive to your needs and company culture.

The results we've had also prove that Gary is a gifted sales copywriter, just one sales letter he wrote for us added 10% to turnover."

Carole Fletcher & Bob Hart: Proprietors of 'Intuitive Media' BAFTA award winners for their contribution to IT in entertainment

"Gary Courtenay and I have been business partners for almost eight years now and even after all that time he still he still amazes me with the way he can generate idea after practical idea at will. In any business situation he will always bring new and fresh thinking to the table. His marketing style is stealthy, streetwise and often highly unorthodox and many of his strategies have had a huge impact on the growth of the three businesses in our group, contributing massively to over quadrupling our turnover during the years we've been together.

Gary's greatest gift though is as a wordsmith; he has the innate ability to write incredibly persuasive sales copy and now the even rarer gift of being able to teach that to others.

I probably shouldn't have been surprised that Gary has also emerged as one of our country's best business speakers, he has shown himself to be an awesomely powerful communicator with the ability to inspire everyone in an organisation from the CEO to the cleaner. I can vouch for the fact that many of Gary's key marketing principles are in his book and you will learn a lot more than just 'how to write sales letters with clout' when you read it."

Ken Eddie, CEO – Nutri (Imports & Exports Ltd), CEO – Diagnostic Services Ltd, Director – Mentor4business.com

"I have been bowled over with your enthusiasm, drive, insight, knowledge and expertise. Without exception I have received compliments from the team about your talks at our last two sales meetings at which you have spoken. I for one gained as both a salesman and a manager from the powerful knowledge and tips you had to share with us."
Andrew Hayhurst – Regional Sales Manager – The Black & White Mortgage Company

"I am pleased to recommend your services most highly. Your knowledge and understanding of so many marketing concepts is unrivalled and since you have also implemented many of these ideas yourself, they come with relevant suggestions for implementation. Your service is in my opinion the quickest and most cost effective way to grow the turnover and profitability of a business."
Adrian Williams CEO – Scenic Maps Ltd

"Gary, on a personal note, you have been an inspiration and mentor to me, your ability to listen, encourage and coach at all times has benefited me every time we meet."
Mark Boxall, Director – Chapter 26 – IT Consultancy

"Many thanks for the recent marketing and media seminar for my executives. The marketing section was extremely valuable and provided us with numerous useful strategies.The feedback I've received is excellent and shows that all the delegates found the time they spent with you both rewarding and enlightening."
Mike Brown CEO – Fylde Borough Council

"Gary – this is to offer our thanks for such a great presentation yesterday. The comments and reaction from our members confirm that you did indeed deliver a stimulating and motivating presentation. There certainly aren't many orators around who can present with passion yet provide such solid material for their audience."
Ken Griffiths Chair, Trafford Business Club

"Due to the time I invested in spending with you my business has now catapulted to a new level and already I have paid for your fee at least 10 fold. My only criticism is that for your own sake you should and easily could charge more."
Charles Ferguson – Solicitor Advocate

"Your marketing advice has been a great help – very specific and often pointing out opportunities that sometimes seemed obvious and yet no one else had spotted them. Because you were specific we have found many of them easy to action."
Ian Henderson – CEO Wyre Housing Association

"I am writing to thank you for the consultancy work you carried out for us. As you know, we took up many of the marketing suggestions made in your initial report. And applied them, with great success. In particular your recommendation for acquiring referrals and leveraging this with an incentive gift provided particularly powerful results. Once again many thanks for your input, I look forward to working with you again in the future."
David Hughes – CEO Nightingale Conant – UK leading publishers of business and self-development material

How to Write Sales Letters with Clout

"There are two types of knowledge.
One is knowing a thing,
the other is knowing where to find it."

– SAMUEL JOHNSON

Benjamin Thomas Corporation

Published by Summertime Publishing in association with the Benjamin Thomas Corporation

ISBN 0-9529453-8-X

Author:	Gary Courtenay
Editor:	Jo Parfitt with Fiona Cowan
	www.summertimepublishing.com
Cover design:	Gary Courtenay
Interior design:	Wendy Barratt
Print and production:	White Label Publishing

About Gary Courtenay

Gary Courtenay currently sits on the board of three companies and is the CEO of M4B (mentors4business.com) a company that helps mentors and mentees find each other. M4B also provides a host of business development products and services to the UK business community.

With over 25 years experience in business, Gary was recently invited to lecture on sales and copywriting at the world renowned Cranfield Business University.

A popular and sought after speaker, Gary provides a range of keynote speeches for UK businesses and organisations. He has headed up many companies during his career where he has always taken the responsibility for sales and marketing as a means to drive the business forward.

In recent years he has worked with his business partner, Ken Eddie, in the Peak District, where together, they have grown two health care companies to around four times their size in around six years. Nutri Ltd, specialises in the supply of the highest quality nutritional supplements to health care professionals. The other company, Diagnostic Services, supplies the same customers with a range of hi-tech, ground-breaking diagnostic services in association with the internationally acclaimed Great Smokies Diagnostic Laboratory in America. You can visit Nutri's website at www.nutri.co.uk

Gary has lived most of his life in the North West of England and currently lives with his wife Janet and son Ben in Medlar-with-Wesham, a village in the countryside, west of Preston, Lancashire. Gary's hobbies are writing, travel, photography and spending 'quality time' with his son Ben.

Dedication

I dedicate this book to my magical little boy, Ben, whose special presence in my life provides me with my main reason to be here, as well as all the fun, companionship and motivation I could ever wish for. I also dedicate this book to my wife Janet, who has supported me and stood beside me for over 20 years and faced all the challenges life and business have thrown at us.

Acknowledgements

There are many I should thank, but top of the list should be my good friend Chris Payne (of Life Tools). With my interests at heart Chris wickedly made the whole process of writing and producing a book sound so simple and easy I could not resist going ahead. In the event, his advice and insights have been invaluable. Thank you Chris.

I have had many business partners over the years and Ken Eddie is the best, the most decent and the most honest of them all. Not only did Ken immediately see the merit in this project but he has enthusiastically supported me too, especially through the many hours it has kept me away from the office and my role of Group Marketing Director within the Nutri group of companies.

Colleague, Mark Kelly, also played his part by constantly insisting that I should somehow get my knowledge into a book. It's possible that Mark was the catalyst for my at last beginning this project. UK speaker and motivational expert Nigel Risner also gave excellent advice, and as ever, was generous with both his support and his contacts.

To my dear friends Bob Hart and Carole Fletcher. We have been friends through thick and thin and they have always been a huge inspiration to me. Bob and Carole and their team were also instrumental in coming up with the name Mentors4business.com and in building and launching its excellent website which is powered by their amazing flexible Take2theweb site building technology.

My proper appreciation goes to my editors and contributors Jo Parfitt and Fiona Cowan, who worked tirelessly on my behalf. Jo even worked through illness and their guidance, ideas, feedback, praise and fascination with the content were an unending source of inspiration. In addition, Jo's continuous enthusiasm as the book developed has been positively contagious.

My wife Janet, deserves my thanks too, not just for endlessly suggesting titles for the book, but for putting up with my characteristic single-mindedness, when I am immersed in a big project that excludes almost everything else. Janet also holds down a full time executive position, looks after our home and is the best Mum in the world to boot. Despite living with her I still don't know how she does it all.

I also want to thank my ten-year-old son Ben. He was the first to say that he would buy my book (with his pocket money) from the shop as soon as it came out. He didn't realise he could get a copy from me and thinking about Ben's desire to own a copy of my completed book motivated me more than anything else to get it finished.

Finally, I want to thank my parents, Anne and Derek Courtenay, who are sadly no longer with us. Their unbridled enthusiasm and admiration for my writing skills from an early age served to stimulate both my confidence and my interest to write more and more. It's possible that without their profound encouragement this book would not exist today. I would give anything right now to be able to hand them each a copy and watch their thrilled response.

Foreword by Peter Thomson

I first met Gary Courtenay in 1995 at a marketing seminar for which I was the Master of Ceremonies. Gary was one of a number of people at the event who had the opportunity to speak. It was clear to me from the moment he spoke that Gary has a way with words. His unusual and innate ability to make a focused point makes him an entertaining communicator. A born salesman, Gary never fails to back up everything he says with evidence. He also says what he has to say in the shortest time possible in other words – a natural speaker!

It should have come as no surprise to me during the years that followed, that Gary has shown himself to be an excellent sales copywriter too. He can easily apply the same talents I've witnessed many times at the microphone, to pen and paper.

Master the art of writing sales letters

Over the years I have received countless communications from Gary, many of which have been sales letters as part of a mass mailing. The exceedingly high quality of the sales letters has always been sufficient to grab my attention, involve me, make me want to read right through to the end, and most importantly, make me seriously consider the proposition of the letter. It takes considerable skill to achieve this in a sales letter, especially on a consistent basis. There is no doubt that Gary is an accomplished master of the art of writing sales letters that actually do what they are supposed to do and actually *sell*.

I have dedicated much of my own career to promoting the power of communication and to sharing with the world, the communication secrets I have learnt and developed myself. Indeed most of my books and audio sets are about this very subject *(see the Resources section at the back of this book).*

Enables ordinary people to achieve amazing results

Because of my passion for communication, this particular book and its message resonate massively with me. *This book is a valuable business tool that enables ordinary people with ordinary skills to achieve amazing results.* Now you too can capture the raw power of words and forge them into one of the world's most powerful, inexpensive and under-utilised marketing tools – *the humble sales letter.*

This book is aimed squarely at the person who needs to write a sales letter and realises that sales letters provide a considerable but untapped opportunity, but who has little or no idea how to go about unleashing their massive potential.

Contains only the information you really need

The book is deliberately slim and compact and the largely unnecessary detail that pads out many thicker books has been stripped out leaving only the information you really need to know and will actually use. This format will enable you to read the book rapidly and will allow you to dip swiftly in and out – as and when you need to. In fact, I predict you will find it so handy it will likely win a place in the top drawer of your desk or in your briefcase.

Even seasoned sales copywriters will be inspired

During the last century, sales copy writing evolved into a science and much is now known about what works and what doesn't. Despite this pre-existing knowledge, incredibly, Gary Courtenay has brought a much-needed breath of fresh air to the business of sales copy writing. Many of the stories, concepts and metaphors he uses in this book are highly innovative and communicate complicated marketing principles in a way that is remarkably easy and simple to understand. Consequently, I forecast that even seasoned sales copywriters and wordsmiths will be inspired with new ideas and thinking after reading this book.

As a bonus you will also discover this book contains many additional hints and tips on how to improve sales in any business, however large or small and not just through letters and direct marketing techniques. Gary's marketing secrets apply to most facets of business.

You should also be aware that Gary is a streetwise marketer who has tested and honed his skills in the real world. Not only has he travelled the planet extensively to learn from the best, but he has tried and tested the ideas of others as well as his own. This has been made possible by over 25 years experience as an entrepreneur running his own businesses. In this book he shares business secrets that have been discovered and developed by himself, other master sales copywriters and many of the world's greatest marketers.

This slim book has the potential to improve and change your business. In my experience anything that does that has the power to improve and change your life too.

Have an inspirationally enthusiastic read.

Peter Thomson, author of best selling books
CEO Peter Thomson International PLC
The UK's leading business consultancy group.

Contents

page no.

Introduction

The objective of this book is not to make you a master sales letter writer, for that would take years of study and practice. Indeed, if you are a master sales letter writer then this book may not be for you, although I suspect that even you will pick up a few new tips and ideas that justify you investing the necessary time to read it.

A treasure trove of valuable business tips and information

If you either own or are involved with a business you will doubtless be pleased to discover that this book goes a lot further than just advising you how to go about writing sales copy and sales letters. Inside you will find a treasure trove of valuable tips and information on a whole host of issues connected to business growth and development.

ONE OF THE MOST POWERFUL MARKETING TOOLS ON THE PLANET

Indeed, if you are any less skilled than an expert sales letter writer then this book will provide you with some very simple rules and tools that will enable you to improve dull, ineffective business letters. Using the information in this book you will literally transform your efforts into what many of us have discovered to be one of the most powerfully effective marketing tools on the planet and certainly one of the most inexpensive.

Secrets known only to a chosen few

I have been using sales letters for the last 20 years and have frequently seen them generate phenomenal windfall profits and big money jackpots for myself and the others who use them properly. In fact, so many people fail to use sales letters that I often think that they are a secret known only to a chosen few. If you feel that you are not one of those chosen few then read on … I am about to share these secrets with you…secrets that have made a small fortune for both my clients and myself during the years I've been using them.

my promise to you…

JUST ONE MORE THING BEFORE
WE GO ANY FURTHER …

Please be aware that this little book promises either to inspire you to try sales letters as part of your marketing mix, or to help you improve the results you have been getting to date. So confident and determined am I that you will enjoy either one or both of these benefits, that should you strangely, find this book does not deliver on its promise then I absolutely insist you return it for an instant no quibble refund plus the cost of your postage. I have only one condition to this excellent offer. It is that you actually try out the ideas and suggestions first.

THAT'S RIGHT …
If you apply the principles, techniques and methods in this book and you fail to make many times more than the price you paid for it, then simply return it to me for a rapid and immediate no quibble refund.

This book is mainly aimed at the non-professional and is deliberately compact. The direct marketing industry sprang into being in the 1920s and it has evolved from, and still revolves around, human psychology. How much do you think we still have to learn? Not a great deal more, I suspect.

For almost a century people have been studying scientifically what works and what doesn't.

I can vouch for the fact that there is a sea of knowledge out there on direct marketing that would take the novice years to study and even more years to try out. I can vouch for it because I have spent those years myself gaining my own knowledge and expertise. During that time I have sifted through that sea of knowledge on your behalf. I have carefully selected the most important things you need to know in order to improve your results and I have included them in this book. Let me say again, that if you use the information I am about to share with you, then you will soon see massively improved results too.

I am a passionate believer and exponent of the 80:20 rule, or the Pareto Principle as it is less commonly known, *(see Chapter Seven for a full explanation)*. Pareto was an Italian economist who lived in the 19th century. He showed through research that commonly, 80 per cent of any results we receive through doing something come from only 20 per cent of its constituent parts. This book is that rule in action for I have included only the items you need to know to create massive results easily.

The rest of the information will stay out there in that sea of knowledge. There are many excellent and sizeable books available and if you want to become an expert then perhaps you should study them too. Possibly I too will write a book that covers all the angles in the future. However I believe that this slim book you hold in your hands right now provides you with everything you need to know to write *sales letters with clout* and provide amazing results for you and your business.

If you want to upgrade your skills quickly and simply, and get much better results, then you have come to the right place. This book will hold your hand and regale you with stories that will show you how to write massively powerful sales letters. It will also give you scores of valuable tips on how to write good sales copy for any medium.

Most people think they can't write

Not long ago, I was giving a lecture at Cranfield University about writing sales letters. I asked the 40 students at the lecture how many of them liked writing. Out of 40 mature business people, only three raised their hands.

Interestingly, one of those students is running a business producing sales letters for other companies – and even his hand remained unraised.

I then asked that same group how many of them *hated* writing. On this occasion 37 hands were raised.

I was not surprised when so many admitted to not liking writing but I was surprised by another show of hands which told me that these same people actually *hated* writing. This was a revelation to me, probably because I enjoy writing.

Based on this experience at Cranfield University, it is entirely possible that throughout the business population, 37 people out of 40 don't like writing. This equates to 87.5 per cent.

It's different for me. Writing is relaxing. I find it so absorbing that time flies while I am tapping away at my keyboard. A whole day can pass, and sometimes I even forget to eat or stop for a drink.

You probably have a favourite activity which you find so easy and satisfying that time flies. Chances are, though, that it will not be writing.

What if you're one of the 37?

If you do not consider yourself a natural or gifted writer, then I have written this book for you. It contains no preaching. This book will not make you feel inadequate, just because I find writing easy and you perhaps don't.

No, my promise is that I'm going to make writing easy for you too – in fact much, much easier.

I will share secrets with you that I've discovered during the last 25 years in business. I will show you short cuts that will help you to put an effective sales letter together.

Soon you will be able to write terrific sales letters, even if today you don't believe you have the skill.

You may be one of the lucky three

Even if you are one of the lucky three out of 40 who *does* like writing, the tips I am about to reveal will improve your sales letters beyond measure.

With my help, your letters will become even more persuasive, and hit the readers harder than ever, creating results and responses that are likely to be many times higher than if you simply had a go on your own.

Sales copywriters are among the most highly paid people in the writing profession, if not the world. The best in the world can earn as much as £25,000 from writing a single sales letter. The last time I paid another sales letter writer was in 1997 and I was charged £400 each for several one-page letters. It was this that made me truly recognise and value my own abilities. I was convinced that I could write more effective letters than the ones I had purchased. I have since gone on to prove this to my colleagues, my clients and myself. And these days it is not unusual for me sometimes to spend an entire week at a time writing nothing but sales letters for my own businesses and my clients' businesses.

After reading this book, it is my hope that maybe you, and others like you, will go on to make a new career out of writing sales letters. At the very least I anticipate you will gain an extremely valuable new business skill.

Can working writers use this book?

If you are already employed as a sales letter writer, then you will learn how to improve what you already do well – better and faster than before. In addition, this book will doubtless change the way you think about and gather content for your sales letters.

If you don't already know, then you should be aware, that there is a big difference between *general copywriting* and *sales copywriting*. At the risk of stating the obvious, *sales copy* is usually designed to inspire the recipient to take action, in other words to get out his or her cheque book, wallet or credit card for example, and make a purchase.

To summarise, I believe that very few people write or enjoy writing. Of those who do write, only a tiny proportion are capable of adopting a style that will cause a significant chunk of a target audience to take a specific action, inspired by the letter itself.

Considering this, we should appreciate that sales copywriting is a rare and precious skill. Even though I learned that only three business people in 40 like to write, of these I would guess that only one in a 100 is actually good at it. Therefore my estimate is that less than one per cent of even accomplished writers will be naturally and intuitively good at writing effective sales copy.

What is good and effective sales copy?

Sales copy is all about results. Judging by some of the abysmal stuff that comes through my letterbox, even poor sales copy must generate a good enough response to justify its existence.

Take comfort in the statement above. You see, even a bad effort will often be worth the effort. That, my friend, is a very important point to bear in mind when you are considering using direct mail.

EVEN A BAD EFFORT IS WORTH THE EFFORT

Nevertheless, bad or poorly written sales copy is not guaranteed to pay its way. There is an element of risk in every direct mail campaign. *Your goal should be to minimise the risk and achieve the maximum return possible,* based on your investment of time, effort and money. It is not unusual for a good letter to glean as much as six, seven or even eight times the response of a poorly written one. Indeed, if you follow some of the simple suggestions and methods in this book, you too should soon be enjoying dramatically improved results and responses to your letters.

Writing sales letters is nothing more than *salesmanship in print.* In this respect I may have an advantage, having worked in sales and marketing for as long as I have. Unusually perhaps, I see the whole sales process almost as an art form. I can be fascinated by the grace and beauty that is on display when a skilled practitioner of the art is conducting a sale in an elegant style and manner. Indeed an accomplished artist can make the process look and feel almost invisible to the untrained eye.

Unlike many people, I do not believe that the 'gift of the gab' is desirable in a salesman. In my view, it is a handicap to sales success.

Truly great salesmen ask their prospective customers intelligent questions and then listen intently. They listen more than they speak. In this way, they astutely gather information at a verbal and non-verbal level. They discover, subtly, what might prevent the customer from buying, and also what might encourage him to buy.

Like a surgeon selecting the right scalpel to make an incision, the accomplished sales person will make his presentation based on what the customer wants and needs to hear. Commonly, the rest of the information that may be available, is kept in the background, and only produced if either the customer is particularly interested or if it is required to close the sale.

"Shoot for the moon – Even if you miss it, you will land among the stars."
– LES BROWN

The return of respect

There is a new and welcome technique emerging in business, which, like so many others, has landed here from the USA. This technique is called *consultative selling*. Each customer is thought of as a *valued client*. The salesman places himself in the role of a *trusted adviser* and rapidly loses any perceptions of being like 'Del Boy' peddling his latest batch of dodgy goods.

Consultative selling looks set to infuse even more dignity into the profession of selling. Hopefully, it will also lead to a reduction in the number of people who think the *'gift of the gab'* is all they need to be an effective salesperson.

Doing your homework for the customer

In the chapter called *River of Evidence (Chapter Five)*, I suggest methods you can use to present evidence that your product or service 'does what it says on the tin'.

It is both pointless and naïve to expect the person reading your sales letter just to take your word for it and accept the claims you make for your product or service. This is a common mistake and will usually generate a disappointing response. *Your job is to present persuasive evidence in your letter,* proving that your product or service does what it says it does. Then you have to give your customer solid reasons to respond, inspired by both logic and emotion.

Often I talk about the relationship between risk and evidence. When you have these balanced and weighted correctly against 'resistance to purchase' you will frequently find prospects suddenly agreeing to buy. In fact they will often astound you with the speed at which their attitude changes, once you present sufficient evidence and reduce their feelings of risk in any deal or transaction.

My simple test for knowing if you've made your deal or proposition sufficiently attractive is to check whether you can say with confidence to the customer:

"Well, what have you got to lose by giving it a try?"

It seems that some vendors think they can go out to the market with a deal that is essentially poor and still persuade people to buy in vast numbers. The reality is that they will get many times the result if they have a good value product or service to offer that is already highly desirable. In many cases the trick is to spend sufficient time and thought in designing an outstanding offer to add to your basic proposition so that your overall proposition becomes *virtually irresistible.* You will find out exactly how to do this and more in the pages that follow.

As I said earlier, I will gladly issue a full refund, including postage, to you if after trying out my methods and suggestions for yourself, you decide that this book does not provide value.

In addition, I am delighted to offer you a free £100 voucher for any mentors4business.com product or service, including consultancy, sales document evaluation, workshop, seminar or keynote speech.

What have you got to lose?

Gary Courtenay,
Author, Speaker
and CEO of
www.mentors4business.com

Contact him at:
Tel: 08456 634 1400
Email: info@mentors4business.com

"Success is neither magical nor mysterious. Success is the natural consequence of consistently applying basic fundamentals."
— JIM ROHN

CHAPTER ONE
The power of a letter

THIS SECTION INCLUDES:

- A charity campaign proves the power of sales letters
- How sales letters differ from junk mail
- The two types of letter
- Sales letters can look like something else

How a charity campaign taught me the real power of sales letters

In 1995 I became chairman of my local Round Table – Blackpool Progress No 969. I faced two unusual circumstances.

Usually, the Round Table started the year with zero funds. Part of the chairman's job, together with the members, was to raise money to give away to good causes. Incredibly, my chairmanship was kicking off with charity funds left from the previous year. We had a very substantial £2,990 in the kitty.

The second oddity was that our branch was experiencing a critical membership crisis. We were down to just nine members, a figure that threatened the very existence of our proud little club. This new chairman required a solution – and quickly.

A few sleepless nights later I had a brainwave.

What if I could persuade our main local newspaper *The Blackpool Evening Gazette* to join the Round Table in a 'Fix-It' campaign, styled after the famous 'Jim'll Fix-it' BBC TV programme presented by Jimmy Saville?

My idea was that readers would write in to ask our Round Table to perform tasks and deeds. By generating positive publicity in the press each time we gave our money away, we hoped to attract new members to the branch.

It all started with just one 'letter of persuasion'

My letter to the newspaper persuaded the *Gazette* to become our Round Table's partner in this hare-brained scheme, and I was invited to their offices to plan the project. They agreed to one crucial condition: that in each article about our activities they would also publish an appeal for new Round Table members.

The 'Fix-It' campaign became **the most successful community service project in the history of the Round Table movement.** Our Blackpool branch became the first ever to win Round Table's three most important national trophies – and even more incredibly, all in the same year. The campaign and our tiny little club also scooped numerous other local trophies and awards.

Eventually, the Round Table executive committee asked me to write a book explaining how others could replicate our success. Like everything else involved, this project was undertaken on a voluntary basis. I called the resulting book *'Your Personal Guide to 'Fix-it' – The Most Powerful Community Service Project in the History of the Round Table'*.

The first edition of 10,000 copies was quickly used up and a second edition was published in the same quantity the following year.

I am told that Cardiff Round Table received one of the first copies of the book. The very next year, following the book's instructions, they repeated Blackpool's success – even to the extent of winning one national trophy.

Of course, I had no idea that the 'Fix-It' campaign would take off in the way that it did. During that year, my business became 'Fix-It HQ', taking three times as many calls for 'Fix-It' as it did for our normal trade.

Cover of Fix-it campaign book

I should have just pulled out my cheque book

Hindsight is a wonderful thing. It is obvious now that it would have been less damaging to my business if I had simply pulled out the company cheque book and just written a huge cheque to charity. However, at the time, nobody could have foreseen how it was going to snowball.

The campaign evolved

During the course of the 'Fix-It' campaign, it became necessary to write hundreds of letters persuading people to help us in various ways. Some letters were simply aimed at raising money. Many others were written to branch members and past members, seeking manpower for specific events.

After six months, the funds ran out. But the campaign had gathered so much momentum, I decided to use the publicity already generated to persuade local businesses to sponsor specific deeds. They too, could benefit from the publicity machine we had created.

This called for yet another round of letters.

Ironically, it was during this campaign – labouring unpaid for a good cause – that I learned more about writing letters of persuasion than I have at any other time in my life. I seemed to be spending most of my work and leisure time, passionately writing letters for charity.

Many of these letters brought astonishing results and it was becoming clear to myself and others that I had an innate talent for writing. This surprised me, particularly as I was also beginning to notice that very few others seemed to have this same ability.

More than meets the eye

I had been using sales letters for years prior to the 'Fix-it' campaign. However, at the time I was blissfully unaware that there was a massive and developed science that underpins the so-called *art* of sales letter writing. This knowledge can and should be applied to any letter of persuasion, thereby multiplying its chances of yielding the desired response.

When I found out about this vast resource, I started to study the *science* of sales letter writing. I was amazed at just how much I had already learnt the hard way through trial and error. But I learnt more still through studying the work of the masters that could be found in textbooks and also by attending seminars around the world.

Armed with this knowledge, and with the success of the 'Fix-It' campaign tucked firmly under my belt, I began to use my writing skills for commercial purposes much more than I ever had in the past. I was amazed at the results. Even today, I am frequently staggered by the colossal results that can be achieved by a humble sales letter – which in effect is no more than words in ink on paper. Perhaps then, in some strange way, the refinement of this rather unusual skill was my real reward for all the hard work with Round Table? For there is no doubt that in the years that have followed, the ability to write powerfully persuasive letters has made a huge contribution to my own personal success and to that of the companies I work with.

I know of no more effective and economical marketing method to get great business results.

What sets sales letters (and direct marketing) apart from other forms of soliciting business is this: with great precision you can pick off the ideal targets for your proposition.

Provided you carefully choose the recipients of your letters, you can be confident that every single person receiving your solicitation is probably predisposed to wanting your product or service. **Indeed the selection of the list to which you will send your letters will probably have more bearing on your results than anything else.**

Therefore, it is vitally important that whenever possible, you acquire lists of people who actually have some pre-established interest in your product or service. You can read more about mailing lists in Chapter Three.

This is NOT junk mail

Sales letters are getting bad press these days.

Thanks to the mountain of unwanted post that we all receive on a daily basis, we have a pretty low opinion of any mail that arrives in a highly decorated envelope or a plastic wrap.

We mutter 'junk mail' or 'a waste of good trees', and within a second or two the bulk of those sales letters and other direct mail items hit the wastebasket.

Hang on a moment. Did I just write: 'The bulk of those sales letters'?

Indeed I did. Even this morning, I bet that some sales letters actually found their way into your in-tray, or at least into a situation where they will get read, didn't they?

Even though most of the mail finds its way to the bin, we have to admit that some sales letters do actually work. When they do work, they are a powerful and relatively cheap tool that deserves a prominent place in your marketing arsenal.

You won't have to slog like I did

During the past ten years I have spent countless hours compiling effective sales letters. I have agonised over headlines, fretted over content and pored over the results so that I could measure the effectiveness of my words.

Now that I have sent hundreds of different letters, to thousands if not millions of individuals and businesses, I believe I have unlocked the secrets of writing effective sales letters that sell. Letters that sell well and sell quickly. Letters that have made hundreds of thousands, if not millions, of pounds for myself, my businesses and many of my clients too.

Believe me, sales letters are not a waste of trees.

Two types of sales letter

To get started, you need to know what makes a sales letter different. You already know how a business letter differs from a letter you might send to an old friend or a dear relative. But what marks out a sales letter from any other sort of business letter?

Put simply, a sales letter wants the recipient to buy.

A SALES LETTER WANTS THE RECIPIENT TO BUY

I believe there are two main types of letter. There are *letters of persuasion,* and there are *letters that give information.*

We send letters of persuasion when we want to persuade people to buy our services or products – or to buy more than they would have done, without our sales letter. And sometimes we want them to take some other action that may have nothing at all to do with a purchase.

Letters of persuasion

Most of us have sent a letter of persuasion at some time or other. The last time you applied for a job, you probably sent a letter of persuasion. If you have ever written home asking Mum or Dad to lend you some cash, that was a desperate letter of persuasion as are any solicitations to borrow money or perhaps to secure a lease for a property.

There are many similarities between the type of letters named above and a sales letter. Basically, you tell the reader what you want and give them the reasons why he should comply.

Letters of persuasion want the recipient to do something in response.

Letters of information

Whenever I come home from a holiday, a big stack of mail greets me as soon as I open the front door. I have a superb way of dealing with it.

I find the nearest waste paper bin, I grab a sharp knife, and I go through the whole lot as quickly as I can. Anything unsolicited and of no interest goes straight into the bin, often unopened.

Research shows that we make the decision to put something in the bin in *less than three seconds*. That is a spine-chilling statistic – particularly if writing those letters is your job.

But some of your daily mail will be genuine information. A bank statement is a good example of a *letter of information*. It asks you to do absolutely nothing – other than maybe check it, rip it up or file it. It's just information.

Bills, standing orders and documents that do not ask you to do anything at all, except perhaps pay them, are letters of information. We get mountains of them.

The only problem with information letters is that they dilute the impact of any letter that is asking us to do something.

Sales letters in disguise

On my first day working with a new client company, I walked into the managing director's office and sat down. One of the questions I asked the MD who had hired me to help his business, was how the company dealt with new enquiries.

'We send them a letter,' he said.

'May I see it?' I asked.

'Sure,' he said, and asked his secretary to go to the Accounts Department to fetch one.

As I heard the words 'Accounts Department', my heart sank. I kept smiling, however, and read the letter he handed me. It went something like this:

'Thank you for your recent enquiry. We draw your attention to the fact that it will be 28 days before we can supply you on our normal terms as we need to conduct the necessary credit checks. We anticipate that you will shortly have a line of credit set up with us. However, until then we can only supply you with £50 worth of goods, for which we require advance payment.'

The title of the department that sent that letter would have been more accurate had it been 'The Sales Prevention Department'.

'Well, then? What do you think?' the MD asked me.

'Well,' I said clearing my throat, 'I think we can probably improve on this,' at the same time trying to control my dismay and disguise my feelings at the ineptitude of the letter.

In the end we did improve that letter. We replaced it with four welcoming and informative pages telling the enquiring customers about what we could do for them, how we could help them solve specific problems and about how we were unique and different from our competitors. The improvement in results was immediate and it was dramatic.

I did some internal research to find out how many new enquiries were successfully converted into regular customers. That original cold and unhelpful letter had a miserable conversion rate of just six per cent.

The new four-page letter was a properly written sales letter – and conversions more than doubled to 15 per cent. When we added a special introductory offer to that same letter, conversions rocketed to 25 per cent.

We wanted to do better. We paid a telephone operative to follow up the remaining enquiries who had still not responded. Conversions shot up again, to 35 per cent.

Still not satisfied, we switched the operative for a trained sales person. Conversions rose yet again, this time to a whopping 56 per cent.

Those numbers tell an interesting story. The company had been getting plenty of enquiries – but turning only six per cent of them into customers. We changed that result to 56 per cent. That was an eleven fold increase from the same number of enquiries.

The pivotal factor could only have been the introductory letter. By treating it like a sales letter, rather than an accounting message, the whole picture was transformed.

Seven years later, I was recently persuaded to trim the sales letter from four pages to two. The conversion rate fell slightly. I was not surprised – but that's another story.

However, the above example illustrates what a difference a letter can make.

Never underestimate the power of the right words, used in the right way, and used delicately and persuasively. The words you use can change the result you get in all walks of life. Whether it's with your spouse, your boss or your customers, words will change the results.

CHAPTER TWO
Take heart

THIS SECTION INCLUDES:

- Letters are just another way of selling
- Be brave
- The comfort zone trap

Have a go

"Courage is the first of human qualities because it is the quality which guarantees all others"
– SIR WINSTON CHURCHILL

In one way or another I have been a professional salesman for more than 30 years. But it all started long before that.

Ever since my first selling experience, aged 13, the whole process of selling has fascinated me. I have travelled the world to study from the best and I make a point of putting the knowledge I've captured to work for me.

For 15 years I used and honed these skills in my own mail order company. Eventually this business merged with a much bigger company, where direct mail is also the principal form of marketing.

Sales copy writing is nothing more than salesmanship in print. If you truly understand the sales process, and you can write too, then you have a profound advantage and a head start.

Whether you fall into that category or not, this book will help you get tangible results, making the money and effort you invest in your sales letters worthwhile.

Just take a deep breath – and have a go.

A bear tale

When I was 13, like everyone else my age I wanted money. My dad offered to take me somewhere the next day, where I could get all the money I wanted. Who could resist an offer like that? Excited, I asked permission to bring my best friend, Chris Bottomley.

The next day, Dad took Chris and I to the spare bedroom in our house. I had no idea that one of our own bedrooms would be stuffed to the gunnels with soft toys. We had to squeeze in, because it was packed, floor to ceiling, with giant teddy bears. Each bear was about a metre high.

I was confused. What did a couple of young lads like us want with a room full of kids' stuff? My dad must be showing us this for a reason, I thought, but the burning question in my mind at that moment was where the money was lurking.

'There you go,' said Dad, stepping into the middle of the room and opening his arms wide. 'As much money as you want is right here.'

Chris and I shot doubtful glances at each other and then back to my Dad.

'You can have all the money you want if you go out and flog the teddy bears,' he said. 'This is Blackpool, people buy teddy bears.
So it's easy, if you want money, go flog the bears.'

Starting to feel intrigued, I asked to whom we were supposed to sell them.

'All sorts of people will buy them,' Dad answered. 'Just walk up and down the Golden Mile.'

For those of you who do not know, Blackpool is a big seaside resort with a thriving funfair. In the summer months it is packed with tourists and holidaymakers. The Golden Mile is the promenade that runs from the Tower to the Central Pier and it is filled with shops, ice cream stalls and amusement arcades. Every year Blackpool receives an incredible 17 million visitors.

I trusted my dad, but I still did not understand. Dad was suggesting that Chris and I go into pubs and persuade the publicans to buy the bears for their raffles. He also said we might sell them to Working Men's Clubs and the like.

There we were, just 13 years old, being told to walk into places where you had to be 18 to buy a drink and at the busiest time of the year. Luckily I was tall for my age – just under six feet. Anyway, after a quick chat, Chris and I decided to give it a go.

Taking the plunge

That evening we went out with two bears each. Those things were so big, we could only carry one under each arm and I'll always remember that although they weren't heavy, strangely they made your arms ache trying to grip them. Of course, at that age we couldn't drive. We couldn't even get on a bus with such huge creatures under our arms, so we decided to walk the mile and a half towards town calling in pubs on the way. Eventually we came to a pub called the Sherbourne Arms, on Sherbourne Road in the North Shore area of Blackpool. We stood outside that pub for about ten minutes, squabbling about which of us should go in first.

'Go on then – you go in,' I said to Chris.

'Nah, you go in,' he replied, looking nervous.

'No, you,' I repeated. And on it went until eventually I took a deep breath and said: 'Oh, come on, what's the worst that can happen?'

With that I elbowed my way through the door with the a teddy under each arm.

My dad had suggested we start by asking to see the landlord. Never having been inside a pub before, we marched straight up to the bar.

'Could I see the landlord?' I squeaked and then hastily cleared my throat.

After what seemed like an eternity the burly landlord appeared in the bar to be confronted with two spotty kids clutching outsized teddy bears.

'Yes,' said the landlord quizzically in a very deep voice.

'Do you want to buy a teddy?' I asked, trying to disguise my terror.

To my utter amazement, the landlord smiled, then laughed and said 'how much?' When I told him he reached for the till, right there and then, and said, "I'll have two". With no further persuasion, he bought our first two teddy bears.

'I'll have them for our raffle, lad,' he said gruffly, and paid us three pounds cash on the spot. Our profit on each bear was 15 shillings, the equivalent of 75p today.

That night, our first day in sales, we had to return (with aching arms) to my dad and that spare room for four more bears because we had sold out. Yes, we hit the Golden Mile and eventually sold the lot. That first evening we earned ourselves an incredible three pounds profit apiece.

This was not my only source of income at the time. I was doing a paper round, morning and night, as well as a butcher's round all day on a Saturday. All that hard work was earning me less than £2.10s a week (£2.50 today).

After that first evening I went home and looked at all my lovely money. It was a fortune, enough to buy a pair of Levi's – and I'd made it in *just one night*.

That was a defining moment for me. I have been hooked on selling ever since. By overcoming my fears, and daring to burst out of my comfort zone, I earned a week's money in one night. The two big lessons for me?

1. There is easy money in selling if you have a reasonably desirable product.

2. There is money to be made for those who can overcome their fear and force themselves to do that which is either uncomfortable or even frightening.

Dare to leave your comfort zone

I'll let you into a secret: I have never come across an easier way of making money than by just selling things.

Here's another one: you don't need the 'gift of the gab' to sell things. You do not need to be brilliant at collating and compiling what I will later describe to you as *'The River of Evidence'*. There is just one thing you need, in order to be a good salesman:

YOU NEED TO HAVE
'BOTTLE'!

All you need is the courage to have a go. Once you are prepared to give it a try, and you are set up with decent products or services at a competitive price, usually there will be customers for you to sell to if you will but try.

Substantial and sustained success almost always lies beyond your 'comfort zone'. You have to force yourself to do things you would prefer not to. This idea is so powerful, I have turned it into a separate keynote speech, which I often deliver called *Beyond the Zone*.

The bottom line is that you have got to summon up the bravery and just *have a go*. Stop telling yourself that you can't do it. To my mind, the absence of self-belief is the biggest obstacle to personal achievement.

You can do this stuff. It is not witchcraft. Nor is it rocket science.

And selling face to face is not so very different from selling by letter of persuasion. You just have to learn how, and then do it.

"Courage is the mastery of fear,
not the absence of fear."
– MARK TWAIN

CHAPTER THREE
Snatching good ideas

THIS SECTION INCLUDES:

- Detective work
- Questions
- Who are you writing to?
- Mailing lists
- What do you say?

Don't junk the junk

I am going to suggest you do something that is clearly mad.

Think about the quantities of *junk mail* that you throw away at home and at work every day. The mountains of unwanted, useless correspondence that stops you from getting on with your work.

My word for this material is SNATCH. Here's what I do with it:

Right next to the place where I open the mail, I keep a large file labelled in big black letters with the word SNATCH. Any letter that I receive, that stops me just long enough to make me read it, I keep in the SNATCH file. I also put any other mail that I find of interest in it too.

You should start your own SNATCH folder right away. When you have amassed a big pile in your file, it is time to take a closer look at what is in those letters – and identify what exactly made you pause.

Even better, try to collect samples of good sales letters from a range of different industries. What you are creating is your own resource centre, which you dip into whenever you are looking for ideas and inspiration so that you can *snatch* some of the best ideas just when you need them.

You are not being a thief – just a detective. It is quite legitimate *research*.

I don't want to shatter your illusions – but even the best sales copywriters crib ideas from other letters and good copywriters. So start filtering your *junk mail* from now on. Look afresh at other people's sales letters and the bits and pieces of direct mail that you receive. Evaluate it and then 'snatch' the best ideas to adapt and adopt for your own use.

Questions, questions, questions

You may not have realised it but we all ask ourselves questions as we go through the day. These questions help us make sense of life, enable us to determine what work to do, help us prioritise what work to do next and who to see next. We subconsciously ask ourselves these kinds of questions before we undertake any activity that is not spontaneous.

The key word here is *evaluation*. Even when you open your *junk mail* you are evaluating for an instant whether it might be something you need to read or not. If the mail gets a 'not' then it goes straight in the bin.

Now that you are going to be a master sales letter writer, you need to start asking yourself a new question. Get into the habit of reflecting a second or two longer. Consider whether that piece of mail has anything you could adopt and adapt to use in a sales campaign of your own. If your examples come from a different industry, this will be all the more effective.

The SNATCH habit requires no writing skills whatsoever and only needs you to develop the habit of filing the snatch in a handy place. You can start making it work for you today. Start adding to your understanding of the difference between good copy and bad. If a sales letter tickles your fancy and tempts you to read further, put it in the file. One day, when you are ready, you may be able to use it.

Who are you writing to?

Now for another tip. Let's think for a moment about these *letters of persuasion* and ask ourselves what they can be used for.

They can be job applications. They can be used to sell things. They can advertise special offers and promotions. They can launch new products or tell clients about a new catalogue or a new store or something new that your business now has to offer.

And then there is the big one, the biggest reason of all – the letter of persuasion that is used to recruit *new customers*.

Mailing lists

Lots of businesses buy or rent pre-established mailing lists. The people on these lists are certified as being predisposed to buying certain types of products or services.

Often these lists are costly. One I was considering just the other day was on offer at £140 for every 1,000 names – and with a minimum purchase of 5,000 names. But although expensive, it is well documented that the quality of the mailing list makes a crucial difference to the success of your campaign.

I should say the subject of sourcing and buying in specialist lists and the management of data is highly specialised. It is not the intention of this book to go into this area in great detail, but if you are reading this book, it is assumed that you will already have a project and a selection of prospects to write to.

Some people would say that your mailing list is the most important factor when it comes to writing winning sales letters.

It stands to reason that no-one will buy your product or service, however good it may be if they simply have no need for it or no interest. You are unlikely to sell double-glazing to someone who rents his house for example. You are unlikely to sell a motorbike to someone who is bedridden, but there will be exceptions of course.

It only makes sense to mail the people who have already bought or who are predisposed to buying the kind of thing you are trying to sell.

Mailing lists can be used to help you to target these customers specifically. You can find lists that will locate them in your area, for example, or nationally. You can buy lists according to demographics, age, income, marital status or occupation. You can also buy them according to the interests of the addressees. These addressees will have been sorted by such things as hobbies, the publications they read and the sort of things they tend to buy.

There are two main types of mailing list. A *compiled* list is rather like a directory or telephone book. A *direct response* list is more specific and includes people with a proven history of buying through the mail before.

Lists can be rented through list brokers targeted according to your exact needs. It is obvious that *direct response* lists will out-pull compiled lists. But sometimes you may have a job getting hold of direct response lists for your business.

What do you say?

So, you have your list. The next thing you normally do is to write to the people on the list saying words to the effect of : 'Why don't you do business with us?

And then you try to persuade them to do so.

As simple as all this sounds this is arguably the single biggest reason why companies send out sales letters. You may be interested to know that the average response rate in the UK for direct mail is currently around four per cent.

This seemingly small percentage rate is not a reason to give up on this type of sales letter. Your aim should be to do much better than this and you will if you follow the advice in this book.

CHAPTER FOUR

Beating 'buyer beware'

THIS SECTION INCLUDES:

- Caveat Emptor – your enemy
- So why are prospects suspicious?
- Credible sources of information
- Evidence
- Proof

Caveat emptor – your enemy

This chapter can be summed up in two words: *information matters.*

Like SNATCH, information provides *evidence* that will make your sales letter irresistibly persuasive.

In the case of sales letters, that information could be a testimonial. A glowing recommendation from a satisfied client provides evidence that your product or service does what it is supposed to do. Using the testimonial of a satisfied customer will help to persuade other potential clients that we are good at what we do. You will find a selection of extracts from my own testimonials at the start of this book.

There is an age-old saying, dating back to the Romans. You may know the Latin phrase *caveat emptor*: 'let the buyer beware.' The phrase may be 2,000 years old – but time has not eroded its powerful message.

So why are prospects suspicious?

At some time in your life, you may have walked through a shopping precinct or attended a trade fair, and come home afterwards with one of those handy little machines that chop vegetables in numerous different ways with apparently little effort.

I bought one once; it was called an AutoChop. At £4.95 it seemed relatively cheap and like many others in the crowd I bought one on impulse. It was the demonstration that really persuaded me, and I watched in amazement as the vendor pumped vegetables through the machine at lightning speed, and produced astonishing quantities of little chopped bits that made huge and decorative piles.

It was impossible not to be impressed by such a clever gadget, requiring neither batteries nor electricity. The demonstrator drew attention to the fact that he only had six machines left,. I bought one at the end of his pitch with about twenty other people as the price was reduced in stages from around £20 to 'just a fiver to clear out these last few'. When I got it home, I couldn't wait to get it out of its box. You can imagine my disappointment when I tried it and found it fairly useless. I had more chance of chopping my fingers than the vegetables.

We've all done it – bought something on impulse that doesn't seem as beautiful or useful once we get it home.

Thanks to AutoChop and similar experiences through the ages, human beings have learned to be very, very suspicious. We have developed a healthy scepticism that leaps to our defence whenever people try to sell us something. It is there to protect us from bad buying decisions. This caveat emptor attitude is so much part of our society and culture these days that many of us are suspicious and cynical about merchandise at a subconscious level.

HUMAN BEINGS ARE VERY SUSPICIOUS

Credible sources of information

Let's imagine that you want to buy a car and are standing in a showroom, looking thoughtfully at one particular model. You are approached by a salesman, who gives you a guided tour of that car.

Are you going to believe everything the salesman says? Or do you decide, before he even sidles up to you, that you are going to be sceptical about everything he tells you? Have you already decided this approach, before the salesman gets to speak a word?

We need to understand what makes the difference between professional business people like you and me, with a great product or service to sell, and the stereotypical car salesman whom we often distrust even before we've met him.

I suggest that we have a lot in common with that poor beleaguered car salesman.

We have good products, we offer good service, and we are trying to sell to people. We want to tell them good things about our products or service. Yet our potential customers are going to look at the information we give them sceptically. People are likely to feel the same way about your product, as you feel when you are being sold to by a car salesman.

By the way, if you are reading this and work as a car salesman, please don't take any of this personally. I am borrowing a cliché to make a point, and you too will benefit from the techniques I am about to share.

Evidence

Let's pretend to be the prospective customer for a moment. You are about to tell your prospects that you are better at what you do than anyone else. Unfortunately your competitors are saying exactly the same thing about themselves.

Think about it. If everyone claims to be the best at something, where does that leave the customer? Probably confused!

This is where evidence comes into its own. It is the magic ingredient we use to counter objections and smash scepticism. We unearth third-party evidence and we reproduce it in our sales letters. That's what testimonials are for. Testimonials say that what we are offering is the best for that real life customer.

Start hunting for your own evidence.

Where do you find evidence?

Look out for research and academic studies that back up what you say. Quote those statistics in your sales letters. Mention the university, or the name of the professor, author or journalist who has written exactly what you want your customers to read or hear.

When you state a fact that will help to persuade your customers to buy from you, you must remember to quote the source. Mention the name of the journalist and the publication that included your important fact. It lends credibility to the statement – as well as keeping you on the right side of copyright law.

As you start to incorporate these things into your sales letters, two things are going to happen. First of all, your letters become easier to put together. You can take the words right off one page, and put them straight into your letter.

Importantly, the other thing that will happen is that your letter becomes much more interesting to the reader.

Proof

Let's go back to our cliché car salesman again. Armed with the kind of evidence we are talking about, he would not simply be walking you round the car. He would now be in a position to prove that the car is as good as he says. He can prove it is better than another similarly priced model – even a newer one.

Imagine how you might feel if you were walking around the car and the salesman pulled out a copy of What Car? magazine.

'Let me show you this league table, Sir. This model has been voted Number One in its class this year,' he might say.

Or:

'Let me show you this report by Jeremy Clarkson. In fact, will you allow me to give you a recent video showing him driving this car on Top Gear? You can see for yourself what he says about it. Don't just take my word for it,' he may add.

Wouldn't that make a difference to your feelings about the car and what the salesman says about it?

In the example above, he said: **'Don't just take my word for it.'** That's a powerful phrase when used in conjunction with evidence.

I love that phrase. Keep it in your mind when you are writing. Inviting your reader not to take your word for it will inspire you, if not force you, to go and find some evidence that supports what you want to say.

Providing evidence allows you to avoid the *caveat emptor* mindset.

DON'T JUST
TAKE MY WORD FOR IT

CHAPTER FIVE
■ The River of Evidence

THIS SECTION INCLUDES:

- The source of the River of Evidence
- The ten waterfalls
- Lift letters
- How to use evidence to write great copy
- The River of Evidence matrix

The source of the *River of Evidence*

I came up with the *River of Evidence metaphor* back in 2002, during a visit to Niagara Falls. To my surprise Niagara Falls turned out to be not just one waterfall, but *three*, each one gigantic in scale and cascading down to feed to one big pool below that eventually becomes another river.

The crashing water is so thunderous that when you are near it conversation is impossible.

Prior to my trip to Canada I had been mentally wrestling with how to teach the concept of using evidence as part of sales copy. I was also searching for an analogy or metaphor that would make it easy to teach about what constitutes evidence. As I stood there before the mighty Niagara Falls, with the sound of the water thundering past my ears I suddenly saw the parallels between Niagara and the *evidence* you need to put into sales letters. I could see the *River of Evidence* as an enormous river, feeding its own *Niagara Falls* from the top – but which then descends as several separate waterfalls into the river below.

Each of the *waterfalls* you need to feed your *River of Evidence* has been given a name. You have to visit each of these waterfalls, when you are fishing for evidence to prove that what you say about your products and services is true.

Waterfall # 1 – Testimonials

The *Testimonials Waterfall* refers to all the good things other people say about you – most commonly these come from existing customers.

Start collecting all the favourable comments and reports you see. Keep hold of the complimentary letters you receive. Print out the emails and hang onto the thank you cards and the comments on your feedback forms.

Every time I speak or give a presentation, I issue feedback forms. You should do this too. Or, if you don't give presentations regularly or run workshops, create a questionnaire to give your clients at the end of a contract.

Whenever someone thanks you or pays a compliment, ask if they would be kind enough to put that in writing on their own company letterhead. Once captured you can use the things your clients say about you, again and again. Testimonials are usually amongst the best proof available that you really are as good as you say you are.

Waterfall # 2 – Public Relations

When you have any good publicity, capitalise on it.

Really make your PR work for you. The biggest mistake most people make with PR is paying for publicity and then forgetting all about it. To make PR really work for you, you need to go a step further and reproduce any articles in which you appear. Now you need to redistribute that material to anyone who may not have seen it when it was first published (you may need the publishers permission). This method puts you in control of your PR. Used properly it has the potential to put every article in front of more people than when it was first published. You can even distribute this PR to many of your existing customers in order to reinforce their loyalty and belief in your product or service.

Ask your customers whether they saw the article. If they didn't, make a little note and pop a copy in the post to them.

Despite the high cost of public relations, it is a fact that more people will not have seen the resulting publicity, than will have seen it. In-house reproduction, through newsletters, memos and letters, is a cheap way of multiplying and massively capitalising on the impact of your PR.

Recently I did some consultancy work with a company that focuses much of its marketing budget on public relations – yet even they had never thought of this approach. This one method can represent tens of thousands of pounds worth of added value, to a company with a £6 million turnover as is the case with the one I just referred to above.

Waterfall # 3 – Referrals

Another company I work with receives about 20 *passive referrals* each week.

By *passive referral,* I mean referrals that come from people without having asked them to refer prospects to you.

Through asking the right questions we have discovered that most of these *referrals* come from satisfied clients recommending the company to other people. You may find it interesting to learn that this constant stream of referrals adds 10 per cent to the growth of this particular company every year.

Providing you take the time to discover the identity of the people who send you referrals you can then approach them to give you written testimonial too. After all they must be saying sufficiently good things about you to persuade others to seek you out and do business with you. So, in essence, all you're asking them to do when you ask them for testimonial is to do what they are doing naturally anyway.

We are influenced by what people tell us about their experiences. Getting word-of-mouth recommendations to do our selling job for us eliminates a big chunk of the buying decision from the customer. *Referrals* often allow us to glide over *caveat emptor* style resistance effortlessly.

Use your *River of Evidence* in a clever way – combine it with statistics and use them to prove any selling point you wish to make You are now developing a winning sales letter.

Waterfall # 4 – Statistics

People always like to see statistics. It is well worth the effort of digging them out. People can't help trusting published facts and figures. And there are bags of them, waiting for you to find them and help yourself.

Again whenever possible use statistics to prove what you say is true and to make your proposition even more attractive.

Let me give you an example. I frequently work with a health care company and often help them with the marketing of glucosamine sulphate. If you don't know what it is you may like to know that one in three people with joint problems in the UK use glucosamine sulphate.

That is a great statistic. Now if you started having joint pains tomorrow, wouldn't you at least be interested in that statistic? Perhaps you would even think about trying some glucosamine sulphate for yourself?

Turn facts into evidence

Not long ago, I gave some sales letter training to a company that sells adventure holidays to schools. The holidays are aimed both at the school children and the teachers. The company takes big groups to Africa, the Middle East and other exotic locations, where they are often able to camp out in a safely managed setting.

I first went into the company to help them to write their sales letter. I am not being unfair when I say that the letter they had been using before we met was bland.

Bland sales letters do not encourage the recipients to pick up the phone and book an adventure holiday. I asked the client if they could tell me who the brand leaders in his market might be. He told me that *they* were undoubtedly brand leaders.

Next, I asked him how much bigger his company was than its nearest competitor. It was at least five times bigger. To turn this into figures, he told me that they had worked with 240 schools the previous year, when their nearest rival had worked with just 40 or 50.

All I had to do was re-word that sales letter, inserting the *evidence.* I said, perfectly factually, that the previous year four out of five teachers had chosen to take their pupils on adventure holidays with (naming their company), and then I gave the reasons. In fact, these reasons were all the *benefits* of using that company. Many of these benefits were then listed out as bullet points.

It is easy enough to see how the *evidence* was built into the statement. I'm sure you will agree that this was much more powerful than simply stating that they were the best suppliers of adventure holidays.

Waterfall # 5 – Research

Let's take the glucosamine sulphate example a little further.

Imagine your client base consists of highly qualified health care practitioners. They are likely to be heavily orientated towards academic studies. In other words, they like and gravitate towards research. In order to prove how good your product is to this market, you would do well to get hold of some university research papers, industry reports and so on. Mintel and similar surveys which report on markets and their trends can be equally influential. You are at liberty to lift information right out of those reports – as long as you remember to credit the source for it.

It is always better to quote the source of your statistics because it lends credibility to the information. The more you use this sort of material in your sales letters, the more interesting they become to the reader. Everyone likes *interesting* letters of persuasion.

Now imagine you are a possible customer, in a business or profession that has a real interest in glucosamine sulphate. There is a good chance that you will find statistics about this very interesting. When you receive a sales letter incorporating quality information based on real facts, that letter will become more interesting still.

And as sales letters become more interesting, they will naturally get a better response. More of your letters will be read all the way through – and fewer will end up in the bin. Information is valuable and keeps your letters in the in-tray.

Research and statistics are two good reasons why your sales letters should be two, three or four pages long, rather than just one page. Anyone could write: *'here is the new Whizz-bang. Buy it now and here's our special offer.'* This kind of sales letter deserves to be called a 'flyer' and it might well be more effective if it was laid out as one.

There is more about the perfect length for a sales letter in Chapter Eleven.

INFORMATION KEEPS YOUR LETTERS IN THE IN-TRAY

Waterfall # 6 – The Media

Articles published or broadcast in the media are eye-wateringly persuasive.

Has anyone ever written about you, your business, your product or even about your industry? The *whole* article might not have been about you – but a section of it could have been pertinent to your business.

If we go back to our adventure holiday theme let's say we have come across an article in one of the Sunday supplements that talks about how travel broadens the minds of children. It tells the story of how a child or group of children benefited from travelling abroad.

I would photocopy that article right away. Then, if I happened to be promoting, or writing about the product in one of my sales letters, I would add a PS to my letter that looked as if I'd handwritten it. It would read something like this:

PS. I'm just attaching a recent article from ABC Life on Sunday magazine, which I think will tell you more about the experience you and your pupils are likely to enjoy than I can, should you decide to join one of our adventure holidays.

What a great example of *River of Evidence* that is. The reader will get the message about the holidays, more than ever. That media article will have more pulling power than anything you could write yourself.

Of course, you do have to be circumspect about what information you include. You certainly don't want to get yourself caught up with lawsuits about Trading Standards or Copyright and it always pays to get the written permission of any publication before you reproduce it.

But you should get into the habit of keeping alert all the time for *evidence* you can use. You will be inspired by all the articles you can get your hands on that concern elements of your product or service, and, this will improve your sales letters immeasurably.

Open a new folder for this kind of information. I find an A4 lever arch file is best. Label each clipping with the publication name and issue date, and put it inside a plastic see-through wallet to clip into the file. The fatter your file, the more easily you will find it to write your sales letters.

Be alert

From now on, stay permanently on the lookout for material you can use. If it works for you, maybe you could keep this evidence in your SNATCH file too. When you spot an article in a newspaper that mentions something important about your product, this is phenomenally useful.

Imagine that you were a car salesman specialising in TVRs, and you saw an article in a woman's magazine saying that women were buying sportier and faster cars these days. That would help you persuade a female customer to go for your turbo cabriolet version rather than the family sized diesel saloon.

You don't need to photocopy the whole article and re-use it in its entirety in your marketing. Just lift a short but pertinent quotation.

Do remember the value of being able to say something like *'as quoted in October's Saturday Telegraph by top columnist Jo Mellor...'*
This is not stealing, nor is it forgery. If the information is in the public domain you are perfectly at liberty to reproduce short snippets in your own material – as long as you quote the source.

Sometimes you may find an article debating an issue that concerns your product. You might not wish to reproduce the negative things the author has written about your product – but you will want to use the positive references. Well, go ahead and cherry-pick the sentences you need, and string them together with ellipses between them . . .
like this.

Use your *River of Evidence* material to influence the way your clients will think about things.

Waterfall # 7 – Quotations

Another useful tip for both writers and non-writers is to quote famous people.

The longer ago they died the better. The more famous they are, the better too. But being famous and dead for a long time is not enough. They have to have said something useful for your product or service too.

"Proper words in proper places,
make the true definition of a style."
– JONATHAN SWIFT

Waterfall # 8 – Books

Seek out books on subjects connected with your product or service. A furniture salesman will be able to find countless books on interior design, furnishings and homes; many of them will be linked to television series so the author will be famous and doubly credible.

Those who operate in the health products arena will find many publications relevant to this market. Imagine how thrilled you would be to read a journalist in a major paper saying: 'Everybody should buy a digestive product, and that enzymes are the way.' What a gift!

There are plenty of similar examples waiting for you to find them. They may be perfectly linked to your business, and you don't even have to write them.

Your job is to open the book, read it and copy out the odd quotation. Providing you only take a sentence or two, this is legitimate.Take any more than that, and you need to ask for permission from the person who holds the copyright of the work, usually the publisher or author.

And remember to credit the source.

Waterfall # 9 – Endorsement

This belongs in the *River of Evidence* because again it is positive stuff that others say about you so it sways the *caveat emptor* sales resistant mind set. This is also interesting because classical endorsement usually allows a product to be sold for a premium that reflects the endorsement. In my workshop trainings I usually use the following analogy:

Imagine you are looking for a gift for a young boy, let's say a neighbour's child. You wander into Woolworth's and spot a good quality leather-cased football on offer for £9.95. Beside those footballs, out of the corner of your eye, you see another ball on offer for £12.95. The more expensive ball is absolutely indistinguishable from the cheaper one. You pick up the dearer ball to find out how they differ. They weigh the same, the stitching is the same, and they are even made by the same manufacturer. Suddenly, you spin the ball and spot some scrawly handwriting, which looks a bit like it says 'David Beckham'. Clearly, the signature had not been handwritten on the ball. Apart from the signature, which may be a fake, you cannot spot the difference.

When I give my workshops I ask for a show of hands to see which ball the delegates would buy. Usually almost everybody, picks the Beckham ball. That, my friend, is the power of celebrity endorsement. So you can see in this analogy that just putting David Beckham's name on something has added a whopping 33 per cent to the selling price and even though dearer has made the same item more saleable.

People often ask me if it's worth paying celebrities huge amounts to endorse their products, I think that in most cases it is worth it, yes, providing that the endorsement allows you to make substantial extra profit that you wouldn't have been able to make without them – simple as that!

All the same, endorsement can be achieved more modestly and without celebrities.

Below are just a few examples:

- **Your clients.** Ask your clients to endorse your product or service. Afterwards you get to approach all their best customers after they have first been told how good you are.
- **Your suppliers.** Suppliers can endorse your product or service. Ask them to say how good you are to deal with and why they would rather trade with you than your competitors.

- **Your competitors.** If you sell cheap products then have the people that sell the expensive products endorse you and vice versa.
- **Academics.** Academics who favour you, your product or service, can often be employed to promote you subtly.
- **Media.** *The media can endorse you in some way too. Joint ventures, such as reader offers, are the most common form of this and are probably much easier to set up than you realise.*

Lift letters

I have decided to write about *lift letters* in this chapter because they fit in perfectly with all the evidence you need to collect. At the same time, they are a useful method for getting the endorsements you need *(see Waterfall #9)*.

Lift letters are so called because they lift response. I often use them when there is someone well known to the prospects or customers you are writing to who will agree to endorsing one of your products by putting their name to it. It is not necessary for the endorser to be famous, just well known to the customers. Celebrity helps though!

Basically then, a lift letter is usually a letter from someone outside your company who recommends your products or service.

When I use a lift letter I will usually enclose it with my own sales letter. Here are few of the rules I apply to my own lift letters:

- Ensure the person has significant prestige to impress the recipients.
- Ensure the lift letter is on different paper and letterhead from the main letter.
- Always get the signatory's permission and approval of copy.
- Collaborate with the person who is putting their name to it regarding the copy and content.
- Keep the lift letter to just one page unless you've something really special to say.
- Consider using a lift letter to reinforce or supply additional *evidence* for one of the key points of your initiative.

Occasionally, however, it can be effective to enclose a lift letter from the CEO along with your normal sales letter. Perhaps you could start with a heading on it that says something along the lines of:

From the desk of G.O. Getter (The CEO) (his name).

This can be used to add extra impetus to your main sales letter, when someone in the organisation of lower rank than the CEO signs that main letter.

Lift letters can also be used as a part of a concerted and planned campaign and sent after the main mailing has been sent. This *second wave* approach works especially well for special offers and promotional campaigns and a lift letter (postcard or second sales letter) sent say, ten days, before an offer expires drawing attention to the offer termination deadline will frequently trigger a flurry of last minute orders that will more than justify the effort involved.

Waterfall No # 10 Demonstration

Now I have saved the best for last on purpose. Demonstration has all the power of all the other methods in the waterfall put together.

The awesome power of demonstration is summed up rather nicely in the story that follows about the most successful sales letter and mailing project I have ever executed. It was for a nutritional supplement named Similase. The product was meant to help people with gastro-intestinal problems, using the highly concentrated power of its own enzyme content.

I observed that incredibly, it was possible to see the amazing power of Similase with your own eyes. All you had to do was break open a couple of capsules, sprinkle the contents onto a bowl of cooked porridge and stir it in. Almost instantly, before your very eyes the porridge would transform into a watery mass as the enzymes took their seemingly magical effect.

This was a very powerful demonstration. I had many meetings with the team, brainstorming ways to show the porridge demonstration to their customers.

Eventually we came up with the idea of posting out a packet of porridge to their top customers along with free capsules of the product in a trendy 'click-pack' pocket or handbag size container. This was accompanied by a four-page letter, printed on glossy A3 paper that folded into four A4 size sheets.

Importantly, each pack of porridge was labelled with clear and precise instructions – and described the sensational result to be expected from the experiment.

Here is what was printed on the label, exactly as it appeared:

> ## Test Similase for Yourself!
>
> Just add 5 fl oz of hot water to the contents of this package. Ensure the oats are thoroughly cooked. Break open 2 capsules of Similase and sprinkle the powder over the oats – watch what happens! Literally within a few seconds, the glutinous mass of oats will transform into a light, watery liquid.
>
> This is a reflection of how Similase acts in the digestive system – bringing its powerful enzymes to bear on difficult, problematic substances.

One other thing about this mailing was unusual. We sent the whole thing out in a Jiffy Bag. This made it stand out from the many A4 and A5 printed envelopes that their customers were used to receiving from us and everyone else.

We ran the promotion for three months. During the campaign, we offered more porridge test kits free and additional capsules to anyone who asked for them.

With promotions like these, I will tolerate losing money during the promotion period, in order to make the money back later on the increase in residual sales. In essence the increased long-term sales revenue should cover the high cost of the promotion.

In this particular campaign, we made an impressive profit on the promotion itself, and, after the promotion had ended, residual sales settled at around five times higher than before we started. **Quite an incredible uplift!**

This gave me one problem. When I see a huge success like this, I want to know exactly *why*, so that I can repeat it. In direct marketing, testing is a wonderful thing. But unless you test in isolation you cannot be certain exactly which element affected your results.

Was it the Jiffy Bag? Or the four pages of A4? Or was it the huge lump in the envelope that generated curiosity and attention?

In the years that followed, I have been able to talk with several recipients of that mailing, and I now know that its success was due to the power of demonstration.

SUCCESS WAS DUE TO THE POWER OF DEMONSTRATION

Don't take my word for it

As you already know, I am a big believer in giving your prospective customer proof that your product does what you claim, and that it will deliver the benefits you describe.

By enclosing a free bag of porridge in the Similase mailing, not only did we stimulate curiosity and command attention, we also allowed the recipient to do his own demonstration and prove to himself that it works.

You see we didn't just ask them to 'take our word for it'.

No evidence is more persuasive than the power of demonstration. Demonstration is the ultimate evidence that what you say is true, and that your product or service really 'does what it says on the tin'.

There is one other charming aspect of demonstration that is often overlooked: executed perfectly, demonstration can often be hugely entertaining. Good entertainment grips the audience, and rivets their attention just where you want it. Above all, it gets them *involved*.

Would you like your own copy of the Similase mailing?

If you would like to receive your own personalised copy of the Similase mailing, complete with porridge, just contact me by email at info@mentors4business.com or telephone me on 08456 634 1400.

Aim for involvement

I often run workshop based training sessions. It always amazes me how much better my students learn from workshops compared with other methods. Clearly, *involvement* has an unbeatable power to teach and establish knowledge. This suggests that *involvement* should be a key ingredient in every demonstration. And it should also be written into good sales copy whenever possible.

The most effective leaders of people are *involvers*. They have the knack of involving their teams in anything –from the decision making process, to being responsible for important projects and systems rather than just for simple one at a time tasks. Similarly, you usually see that successful parents maintain a special involvement and closeness with their children.

Involvement is an influential element that runs through our society wherever a high level of success is present.

The destination: Lake Word of Mouth

Let's take another look at the illustration that begins this chapter.

In summary, the *River of Evidence* runs down in several waterfalls and flows into one big lake at the bottom. I call this *Lake Word of Mouth.*

Lake Word of Mouth consists of *all* the evidence about your product or service that you do not say yourself. It is all the proof, the demonstration, the media, the quotations, the public relations, the testimonials, the statistics, the previously published positive comments and so on that help you to banish the *caveat emptor* effect and get that sale.

You can sum it up in this one simple statement:

> *"The River of Evidence is all the positive things that are said about you, your product, your service and your company that you don't say yourself."*

The trick is to dig out and capture anything that falls into this category for potential use in your sales copy.

Whenever possible use all that positive proof in every piece of advertising. This includes your flyers and your brochures too.

To write advertising copy requires a more disciplined process than writing sales letter copy. For example, an advertisement usually has a non-negotiable constraint on the number of words that will fit on the page or in the advert. However there is no reason why the *River of Evidence* and *Lake Word of Mouth* should not be used to full effect in all your marketing materials.

It is a fact that technology has made it easier today then ever before to produce documents. Now you *can* write sales letters, just by accessing the Internet and doing your research there. You can find articles, statistics and information that you can then use in your sales letters. Be careful to quote the source of any quotations or statistics that you find, and watch out that you do nothing that could be deemed to be plagiarism: at the very least it is frowned upon by many professional writers

The *River of Evidence* matrix

I use a matrix I have developed to help me with the process of evaluating what proof there is out there that will help me to market the current project. You are welcome to use it if you wish. Simply take the following page and photocopy and enlarge it as you think appropriate. Now write the name of your project at the top and put a tick or a cross in each of the boxes below according to what evidence is available. Obviously you can keep using the same piece of paper for many projects until it's full.

The River of Evidence	**Project Name**					
Testimonial						
Public Relations						
Referrals						
Statistics						
Research						
The Media						
Quotations						
Books						
Endorsement						
Demonstration						

CHAPTER SIX
The Balance of Power

THIS SECTION INCLUDES:
- The Tipping Factor
- Guarantees
- Risk reversal
- Adding value

The Tipping Factor

We have already explored the rule of *caveat emptor* (buyer beware), which can be summed up as *natural resistance to purchase.*

Figure 1 shows a set of scales, weighted heavily at one end by the effect of *caveat emptor.*

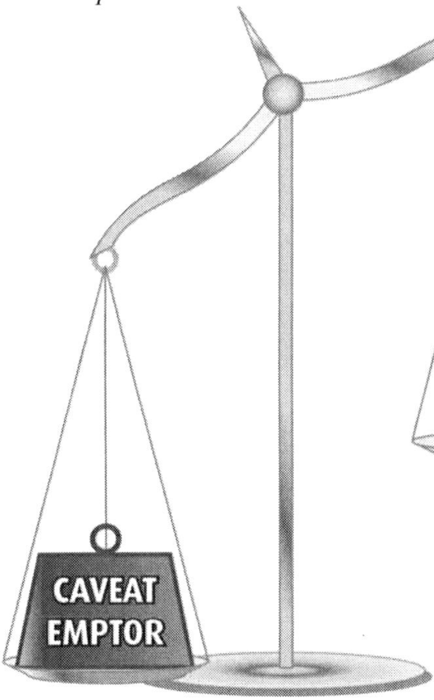

In *Figure 2* that natural resistance is now balanced by the presence of sufficient evidence, that proves the benefits gathered from the *River of Evidence.* As you can see, the balance becomes level.

The Tipping Zone

Every sales professional recognises this situation – where the customer's decision, to buy or decline our wonderful proposition, hangs in the balance. One common clue that this point has been reached is when the customer says the dreaded words:

I WANT TO THINK ABOUT IT

Now lets assume we have already presented all the benefits. We've provided evidence that they are genuine. Yet still the customer won't commit to the purchase. We also know that if we push the customer too hard, we may force him to make the decision we don't want and say: *'No'*.

In this situation, where the scales are balanced, there are a number of ways to tip the scales in your favour, clinch the deal and get that order. Most of the methods I would recommend involve adding value. I will describe a variety of these, but first, I will share with you the single method I have come to trust more than any other:

The guarantee.

Figure 3 shows how you can tip the scales in your favour by combining sufficient evidence with a dynamic *guarantee* proposition thereby beating *caveat emptor* once and for all.

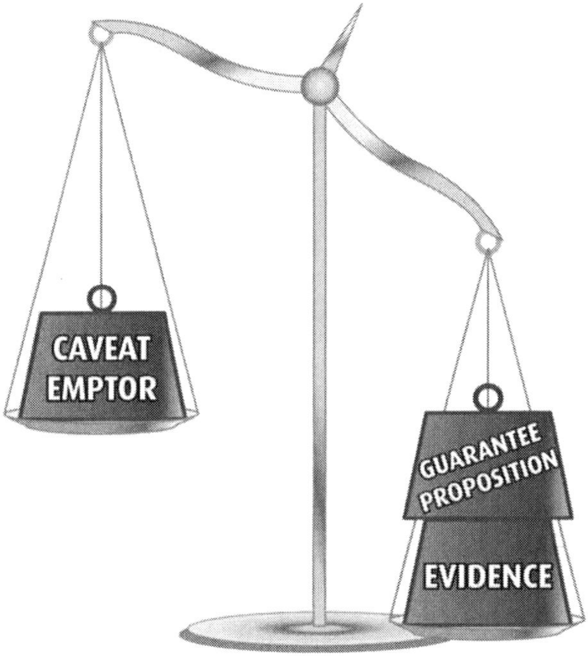

Guarantees

One of the factors fuelling your customer's resistance to purchase will be the risk your proposition holds for him. You must reduce that risk for him, without damaging your own interest in the deal.

By showing that you are prepared to put your money where your mouth is, you create a powerful turning point in the buying decision. Offering a customer his money back, or a free refunds-and-returns service, can tip the scales in your favour.

Not all situations lend themselves to issuing such strong guarantees, of course. Your challenge is to go as far as you dare, in extending the terms of your guarantee in favour of the customer.

The light-switch effect

A good guarantee is often the difference between making a sale and not making one. Radical guarantees are the backbone of the mail order industry. They will offer incredibly attractive terms such as: *'Try it free for 28 days'*. Or even more commonly: *'Your money back if not delighted'*.

I have a colleague called Andrew, whose company sells soft furnishings by mail order, via the Sunday supplements. Recently Andrew discovered that whenever he gave a 'money back if not delighted' guarantee, it added 50 per cent to his sales. When he takes the guarantee out of his advert, its response immediately plummets back to the original level.

‘It’s just like turning a light switch on and off,’ he told me.

Let’s consider this for a moment. Out of several hundred people responding to Andrew’s offer, half as many again *who had previously rejected his proposition* would now say yes – just because of the guarantee. That is a phenomenal turn round.

In direct mail, such guarantees are commonplace. Direct mail professionals have told me they can’t understand how Andrew’s business survived in mail order *without* such a guarantee.

In most businesses, including yours, perhaps, such radical guarantees are not quite so common. The lesson here is that what’s normal in one industry may become radical when applied to another.

What is the risk to your business?

Businesses may be discouraged from making a radical guarantee because they are afraid that customers will exploit it. They fear huge losses owing to returned goods or claims. Such negative thinking stops many of us from putting the persuasive power of a radical guarantee behind our business.

Most companies give excellent guarantees, but keep the fact almost secret. They can't help believing that if the word leaks out there will be a stampede of dishonest people rushing to take unfair advantage.

In fact, the majority of people are honest. Only a tiny proportion will bother to exploit the generosity encompassed in your radical guarantee. The key word here is *proportion.*

There will be some who take unfair advantage, and you should expect this. However you will normally find that the proportion of these people, compared to the huge increase in sales because of your radical guarantee, is tiny.

How do you respond to dissatisfied customers? I am sure you already do something pretty radical to make them happy when something has gone wrong. You probably keep quiet about that, in case others are encouraged to try it on.

Perhaps you don't have a policy about this, and simply negotiate with each aggrieved customer?

I am recommending, as strongly as I can, that you promote your guarantee vigorously along with your goods and services. Save yourself having to deal with *any dissatisfied customers at all.*

Sit down and determine exactly how much risk you can remove from your prospects, to make your proposition so attractive it tips the scales firmly in your favour so that even less of them get into 'The Tipping Zone'.

To get the most out of your guarantees, you must be prepared to honour them. More than that, you have to honour them courteously and willingly, with a smile on your face.

Giving your customer a refund through gritted teeth defeats the purpose.

Once you've established this proposition, then you promote your bold new guarantee prominently, with every product or service you offer.

Let me give you an example from my own life, during the last week or two.

My own scales tipped

I had been away for a few days. Driving home, I decided to buy flowers for my wife. However she has instructed me in the past not to waste my money on flowers at service stations because they never seem to last.

At a service station on the M1 motorway, looking at flowers, I remembered her words. I didn't want to buy flowers there and risk disappointing my wife. A couple of hours later I stopped at another service station on the northbound M6, to buy other things in the shop.

Out of the corner of my eye, I noticed that the flowers on offer had a large sticker saying: *Guaranteed to stay fresh for seven days.*

As you probably know, service stations are not the cheapest place to buy cut flowers. On average, they may easily be more than twice as expensive as you'd find in a supermarket. However, that guarantee tipped the scales and caused me to buy flowers at the service station – when only two hours earlier I had rejected an almost identical proposition from that service's competitor.

Real world guarantees

Here are a few more guarantees and offers that you might be familiar with:

- The mobile phone company O2 allows you to return any mobile phone you take out on contract, for the first 14 days, even if you simply don't like it.
- Domino's Pizza became the world's largest pizza chain by guaranteeing to deliver pizza to your door in 30 minutes or less – or you get it free.
- Argos stores offer a 16 day, no-quibble returns policy.
- With selected clients I will sometimes consult for a day and allow them to pay what they think the day was worth to them, based on anticipated increase to future profits.

In the long run, what would it cost Marks and Spencer to change its policy with regard to returned goods? M&S has built an amazing business on the back of this policy.

Consider the last time you bought clothing there. If you're anything like me, you had that nice secure feeling that you couldn't really go wrong with anything you bought. In fact, I can hear my wife's voice in the back of my mind right now, saying: *'Well, why don't you try it? You can always bring it back if it's not right.'* And you do try it – you buy!

I often wonder just how many additional sales Marks and Spencer makes, because of their radical returns policy. I suspect that, without it, they might not even have a viable business.

Risk reversal

My colleague, American marketing guru, Jay Abraham, has an excellent phrase, which he coined to describe the dynamics of guarantees. He calls it *risk reversal.* Jay offers many case studies where his clients have amassed fortunes by outflanking their competitors with bold – verging on outrageous – guarantees.

Risk reversal is a great name for what I'm talking about. It's self-explanatory.

In essence, you examine what your prospective customer perceives as his risk in your proposition. Then you set about either reducing that risk, or eliminating it.

Frequently, that which your prospect perceives as risk does not coincide with your own view or experience. In these cases you will find it remarkably easy to accept that perceived risk yourself, because you don't see it as a risk.

Thinking about your own business now, how can you tip those scales in your favour and overcome that *caveat emptor/resistance to buy* situation?

One sure-fire way is to offer a radical and outrageous guarantee beyond anything that is standard in your industry *(see Figure 3)*.

Not only will you win a much greater proportion of sales and new customers, you will have the pleasure of frightening your competition half to death as well.

Consider how that guarantee will look in your sales letter. Think about how your customers might feel when they know your product is backed by a cast iron guarantee.

Many people are too timid to return products or make a complaint. You should make it easy for them. One of the best things about guarantees is that if you get them right, it becomes almost impossible to have an unhappy customer.

Statistics show that an unhappy customer will tell seven people about his experience, while a happy customer will tell just three. Use guarantees to ensure you never have an unhappy customer again.

Think seriously about setting up a toll-free 0800 number or Freepost address, so that customers can call you or return products for free.

Make it easy for them. Your reward will be increased sales and a constant stream of referrals.

Don't forget to examine the guarantees your competitors offer.
At the very least, ensure that the guarantee you offer goes further than theirs, to benefit the customer.

Here is a sample of the guarantee used at Nutri, the health care company:

> **The Nutri Guarantee of Quality**
>
> "This is the best way we can underline the confidence we have in our range and how much we value your custom. This is not built on any promise but on absolute trust. So if you or your patient are not completely satisfied with the quality of a Nutri product, simply return it to us within 30 days of purchase. As soon as we receive it we will send you a full refund".

Building an Irresistible Proposition

Great marketers understand the need for an irresistible proposition to help convert even more prospects and minimise the proportion entering the tipping zone. An important thing for you to understand and remember here is that the majority of prospects in the tipping zone usually fail to convert whatever your strategy.

Great marketers spend hours crafting the proposition, which they usually embellish with a guarantee so that the prospect can't see how he can lose even if the item fails to live up to expectations. Even beyond this true masters will often add value, guarantees and evidence, bundling extra items (of a specified perceived value) in an enhanced deal or even free of charge.

Finally the master marketer does not expect his prospect to simply take his word for it that he will receive the benefits as described so hard evidence is provided to convince him that the benefits actually do exist and that he really will receive them.

First, the list of prospects you are approaching is the most important element of your letter. Your proposition comes a very close second. Third, generally the more convincing the evidence you provide the greater the response will be. These are three very simple but important things for you to remember. In the section you have just read I have described in the simplest terms, how you can craft an irresistible proposition just like the master marketers do. This is symbolised in the final illustration of the scales weighed down by all three weights.

Let me give you one very simple example. My business partner Ken enjoys buying fine wines by mail order. One company he regularly uses wrote Ken and told him that due to his loyal patronage they would allow him to purchase a case (twelve bottles) of an obscure white wine for half the normal price (Ken only dinks red) and they would throw in an extra three bottles to boot making in effect fifteen for the price of six. They also said they would take the remaining 14 bottles back and charge him nothing if after trying the first one he didn't like it. Even on this seemingly great deal the wine worked out at over four pounds per bottle. The sales copy did a good job of promoting the wine itself and provided evidence that although unknown the wine was from a renowned vineyard. Well did Ken buy? You bet he did (he bought it for his guests). In fact he was so thrilled by the special offer he assured me he would buy a lot more reds at full price from them in the future. How do you think this company might have gone on if they just offered Ken the wine at four pounds a bottle and simply described it as 'outstanding and great value'? They probably wouldn't have sold him even one bottle. However with the fifteen for the price of six this approach they sold fifteen bottles in just one hit to one customer and left him delighted in the process.

If you use this powerful methodology you will see how you can cause a massive proportion of your target audience to be completely sold and overwhelmed by your deal even before you speak with them.

A good basic guarantee sits at the heart of nearly all successful mail order businesses, many of which rely only on a strong guarantee and overlook the opportunity of offering added value randomly to increase both conversion and response and in such cases such as the one described above, even enhanced customer loyalty.

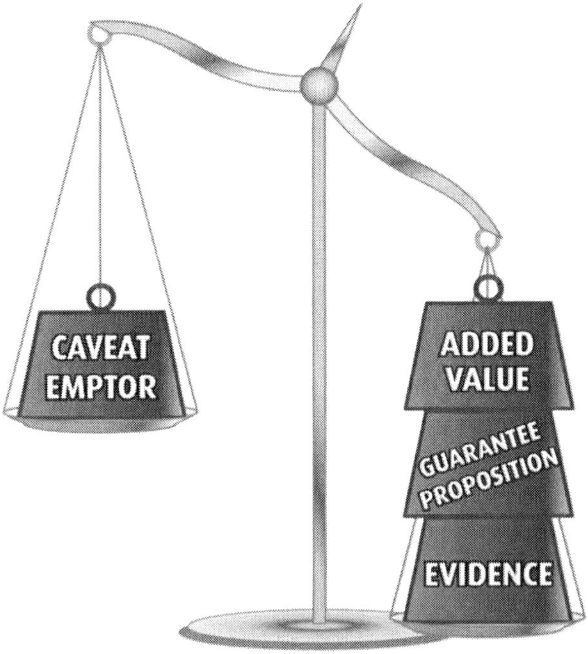

Add value to tip the scales

You can add value to the deal in other ways. This will also tip the scales and cause a sale.

However most of these will usually cost you considerably more than a radical guarantee policy, which sits in the background of your business, working for you around the clock to create sales. Below are just a few I've actually used myself.

Here are a few other ways you might add value to the deal that I have personally used:

- Throw in something free.
- Give a bigger size for the cost of a smaller one (special packs with say '20% extra' free work well).
- Add a service that won't cost you much personally (I sometimes throw in a free follow-up conference call with a consultation).
- Offer a discount.
- Promise money off the next order/deal.
- Don't charge for postage or shipping.
- Include another stock item as part of the whole proposition.
- Fit the product for free.
- Give a free upgrade to a better product or service.
- Buy a certain amount and get an extra amount free ('buy one get one free' – or even 'thirteen to the dozen' – is still an attractive offer that pulls).

Each of the above is capable of tipping the scales and winning you deals and orders that you wouldn't have had otherwise. In many cases you can cost them in at the outset.

Put simply, what I am suggesting is that you make the overall value of the proposition so overwhelming for the customer, he or she just has to say yes. If you do use this type of added value, and it is product, service or discount based, then don't forget to include a cut-off date to stimulate response. There is no law against extending it if you need to.

However, a structured guarantee policy, properly promoted, will have more impact and cost you less in money, time and effort to administer. You can of course mix guarantees with discounts, and even all of this with bonus items – the only limits are your own creativity and your ability to give it a go.

Just in case you're wondering, all of the information in this book about *evidence, caveat emptor,* guarantee propositions and added value apply equally to all types of selling regardless of whether you're in retail, wholesale, manufacturing, direct marketing or any other type of business.

In summary then it is all about crafting the basic proposition of your business and then carefully honing it until your product and service offerings are perceived by your customers as having much greater value than those of your competitors. The end result will be that your business becomes totally irresistible and sales growth soars as a result.

> *"My father taught me to always do more than you get paid for as a investment in your future."*
> – JIM ROHN

A word of caution

As ever in marketing, your byword and your mantra should be: *TEST*. There is more on testing in Chapter Fourteen.

Carefully measure and monitor the cost of claims on your new guarantee and balance these against increased sales. There should not be a problem – but it always pays to know what's going on.

CHAPTER SEVEN

Pack your ammunition

THIS SECTION INCLUDES:

- Why you should make time for preparation
- Benefits and features
- Identifying objectives
- Residual sales targets

Be prepared

Whatever job you do, preparation helps you do it better.

Everyone does it differently, and soon you will find your own way of preparing to write sales letters. However, this is my book, and in it I would like to share with you how I prepare.

Writing a sales letter involves a process, and once you master it the process becomes instinctive. Eventually, you will be able to work less hard at it.

The first thing I do is to discuss the product I am going to write about. This involves talking with colleagues, the client, potential end users, and especially anyone who might influence a buying decision.

This group of people is my *support team*. They help me to identify features and benefits, including those I am currently unaware of, and give me a deeper and more rounded perspective on the item I'm selling.

Benefits and features

Imagine I am selling a technical product. In this case, my first question is:

'What are the benefits of this product?'

Picking out the *benefits* and *features* of a product or service is paramount. Yet people are often confused about them. It would not surprise me to discover that you are sometimes confused about the *features* and *benefits* of your own products yourself.

I frequently sit down with chief executives and company directors who don't know the difference between features and benefits. Sometimes the gap in their understanding is so clear, it's printed in black and white in their past sales letters and advertisements.

Stating benefits is pivotal to advertising and sales letter writing.

People have two fundamental instincts: they want to move towards pleasure, and they want to move away from pain. The *benefits* of a product describe the *pleasure* that the customer could derive from it.

As a potential buyer, with my *caveat emptor* mindset firmly in place, I would want to know what is in it for me if I were to buy this product. What will I get from it, in exchange for my money?

Sometimes people are compelled to do something – or to buy something – purely by their own perceptions. Their motives are all in the mind.

While I'm discussing the product with my support team, and preparing to write my sales letter, I keep the customer and his or her needs at the front of my mind. I put myself in the customer's shoes and ask the 'what's in it for me?' question.

As a sales letter writer, you need to become expert at telling *benefits* from *features*.

How do you tell them apart?

Let's imagine you need to buy a video recorder. You wander into a High Street retail outlet, and an eager salesman tries to sell you a new one. He enthuses about all the VCRs he has on offer. He explains that one especially clever model plays DVDs as well as VHS tapes, has a long play facility, and even has a seven-day timer and a freeze-frame facility.

You might find all this relevant and informative, and feel confident that this is probably the machine for you. Or you might be too embarrassed to admit that you don't know what DVDs are – and unsure about long play as well.

Now let's say that it is not you in the shop with the salesman, but your mother. This changes everything.

What would those features mean to her? They might even confuse her. She may think the machine is too complicated, when all she wants to do is record *Coronation Street* and the other soap operas while she is out playing Bridge or Bingo with her friends.

So, let's re-programme the salesman, to focus on *benefits* for your mother's benefit.

Eager as ever, he explains:

'The feature of a long play facility is that you can use a standard videotape but record for longer than usual. So the benefit of long play is that you can record more television without having to be there to change the tape because it's full.'

Your mother could record a whole evening's soap opera viewing on one tape, and watch it when she gets home from her Bridge party. Or she could happily go abroad on holiday, knowing that she can catch up on the entire fortnight's worth of drama, all captured on a single tape.

Let's go back to our original example – it is you who needs to buy the video recorder. What benefits might the salesman show you?

'You could go away to a conference for a whole week, knowing that every favourite TV programme you're going to miss will be recorded on that one tape. You can then catch up on your viewing at a time to suit you.'

It turns out that 'long play' is not just a feature it actually generates many benefits. It's the salesman's job to articulate these in words and descriptions his particular prospect can understand and importantly, will relate to.

My equivalent job as a sales copywriter would be to turn that mere feature into a *benefit* by writing great, tempting copy describing how you would suddenly be able to relax in front of the television at the weekend after a long week away from home.

Articulating the benefit in this way will relate it clearly to real life. Not just *anyone's* real life, but *your* real life. By doing this, I'm talking about something that's going to enhance *your* life in particular.

This is the real secret of a terrific salesman. He gets his prospective customer talking and thus explores his circumstances, discovers that he is away from home all week, and uses that fact alone to sell him a video recorder that suits him , his circumstances and his real life needs.

Spot the benefit

Perhaps the long play example was too easy. Let's make sure that we thoroughly understand the difference, by examining some of the other features mentioned by the eager salesman – the 'seven-day timer'. How could a feature like that be turned into a *benefit* that your mother would find appealing?

He might describe how your mother would be able to set the machine to record an entire six-episode serial. Every episode could go on to the same tape, one after the other, and your mother could then watch the series consecutively, in one glorious orgy of television viewing. Or she might like to record the whole week's worth of Eastenders.

Now for 'freeze frame'. This is another feature. But freeze frame is of *benefit* if you like sport, and want to see exactly where the ball went. You can judge for yourself whether there really was a foul – or if that ball was offside.

There will be many more benefits than those you first think of. Every customer is different, and each has a different perception of benefits.

The important thing to remember is that *people buy benefits.* Not features.

PEOPLE BUY BENEFITS NOT FEATURES

Practice makes perfect

The other day I saw a superbly written sales letter. It looked attractive, having been professionally designed and printed on embossed paper. But the writer had made a fatal mistake. He believed he had written a bullet-pointed list of benefits – but right away it was obvious to me that his list was of *features*, not benefits.

You must take the time to spell out the benefits of your product or service. Otherwise, you are leaving too much brainwork for the customer to do. Leave him to work out the benefits for himself, and he'll probably switch off. No sale.

Remember this: The benefits may be obvious to you but you are making a dreadful mistake if you just assume they're obvious to the prospective customer.

Benefits first

Lets say I'm working with the health care company I spoke of. Someone walks into my office and hands me a pot of vitamin supplements. It is from the next product range that they are due to promote. The first thing I will do is pay a visit to the nutritionist. I want to hear first hand about the benefits of this product.

'What do these tablets fix, then?' I ask almost facetiously.

Over the years I have tried various ways of asking the nutritionist this, so as to avoid receiving a list of *features*. I've discovered the word *fix* always produces the best result. The nutritionist explains that a person with bad joints, for example, might take one of these pills and get relief from pain.

'Does it fix anything else? I continue.

The nutritionist continues to regale me with a long list of benefits. She goes on to tell me that if I had asthma it could be of benefit when climbing stairs or walking up hills.

Now that I have a list of *benefits* I know what I am going to talk about in my letter.

When I am out collecting information I use a mind map. You may prefer to jot down all the *benefits* you hear about on a notepad. Gather the information in whatever way suits you.

Now start looking for your *River of Evidence* material. Dig up anything that proves these *benefits* really exist. Uncover evidence that proves the benefits work.

Take aim

Once you have collected the ammunition, it's time to think about the target. Your audience.

You need to understand the profile of the typical recipient of your letter, because you have to use the language and writing style that appeals to that type of person.

As Abraham Lincoln said:

'You can't please all of the people all of the time'.

You already know that your letter will be sent to a number of people, not just one individual. Your job is to write for the common denominator. Identify the most typical reader and gear your letter towards him or her. You stand a good chance of pleasing most people, when you write for the most typical recipient.

There is another way of looking at the target audience.

Sniper tactics

You may find it useful to segment your database, in other words, split your database into male and female recipients, or into different age groups, or other categories that seem appropriate for your product. Alas, not everyone has the time or funds to do this.

In the health care business I am involved with, we have experimented with dividing up our databases according to different disciplines. We already know that we serve many kinesiologists, for example, but we also have chiropractors and osteopaths.

The Pareto Principle

We have analysed our database according to the 80:20 rule, which is sometimes known as the Pareto Principle.

Pareto was an Italian economist-sociologist of the late nineteenth and early twentieth centuries. The Pareto Principle states that significant items in a given group normally constitute a relatively small portion of the total items in the group. Sometimes this concept is more commonly called the 80:20 rule.

Thus, in any list of customers, about 20 per cent will usually account for about 80 per cent of the sales. Similarly in a sales force you may well see that 20 per cent of the salespeople account for 80 per cent of the sales. In your business perhaps 20 per cent of your employees may account for about 80 per cent of your absenteeism. Now this principle is not a myth. If you weren't aware of the 80:20 rule already then you will soon start noticing from now on just how it seems to affect almost everything. Once you understand this rule you will see that it has implications in almost every area of your life.

However you should note that the Pareto Principle is a guide. You may analyse your own customer base and discover that, say, 15 per cent provide you with 80 per cent of your turnover. The trick is to understand that it is usually the few (in any list of items) that account for the many. Once you realise where the main cause for something is really coming from you can look at that as a separate segment. Now you can manage and treat it differently in order to either stimulate or reduce the result it creates depending on what it is you desire.

I remember using this technique well in exams by only concentrating on revising for the annually recurring questions which, rephrased each year, accounted for around 80 per cent of the marks. Using this method I was able to pass exams with higher marks than others who had spent many times more hours swotting up on *everything*.

Let me put this in an even simpler context for you. Imagine you had a 'To Do' list with 20 items on it to do today. If you used the Pareto Principle you would look at it and find the four jobs that would give you the biggest return on your efforts. Then you would likely find that these four tasks would generate 80 per cent of the potential results from that list even if you had managed to do all 20 tasks.

The Pareto Principle gives you a very simple method for looking at your customer base and identifying the customers who are doing most of the business with you. Probably these people should deserve some preferential treatment from you. Interestingly, you can sub-divide this elite segment again to create a list within a list. You might wish to label the highest performing segment of this sub list as *key accounts*. At the very least you should study the characteristics of these top performers so that you can establish ways in which you might find more customers like them. At the very least you should be regularly approaching your key accounts and asking for referrals as there is an excellent chance that they know more people like themselves.

In the health care company I work with if we had wanted to compile a mailing that specifically targeted chiropractors, for example, in the past we would also probably have sent much the same mailing to kinesiologists. But then we noticed that our competitors were singling out disciplines and claiming that they had made a specialist range just for them. We realised that, as a supplier, we were being seen as the generalists, while the competitors were seen as the specialists and before we noticed this they had stolen some significant accounts from us using this powerful approach.

Given the right budget and resources, it does make sense to carve up your database and write specific copy and create bespoke offerings according to each market segment. It is the equivalent of the salesman explaining the benefits of a video recorder in one way to you, and differently to your mother.

Just as a point of interest, I was attending a marketing lecture at Cranfield University recently where I was informed that Tesco now have 30,000 segments to their 15 million name database. Tesco's CEO apparently said that running Tesco without those database segments would be like trying to fly a plane without navigation. Evidently this huge amount of data has been accumulated over years on Tesco's incredibly successful loyalty card system.

However you should not worry unduly if you simply do not have the resources or the expertise to market your database in segments. Address the common denominator, and make being a generalist your strength.

Too busy for preparation

You work in the real world, of course. With constraints on your time, action is often a more attractive activity than preparation. However, if you can make the time for preparation, you will get better at it – and faster too. It will save you time in the long run.

Trawl the net

Don't overlook the Internet as one of your most powerful tools. It is a great place to 'fish' in the *River of Evidence*. Try typing your product name or area of business into a search engine. You may be surprised by how many articles have been written – and how many turn out to be valuable.

Anything you read on the Internet is in the public domain. You can copy and paste small sections, straight into your sales letters or print them out for your SNATCH file.

You can take the odd sentence or two directly from the Internet – provided you quote the source.

Reproduced by permission

Once, I saw a fabulous article about fish oils in one of the Sunday supplements. The article was about three pages long, and said everything I could have wished about fish oil. My colleagues in the health care company would be thrilled. I thought it would be a good idea to photocopy the entire article and send it out with a special offer for a fish oil product called Eskimo 3.

Before sending it off, I decided to check that what I was about to do was legal. I telephoned the newspaper and they asked me for £500 for permission to reprint their article in this way.

At the time, the money put me off. With hindsight, I realise that £500 was insignificant compared to the revenue we would probably have made from increased sales.

When you want to reprint an article in full, you do need to contact the publisher for permission. Even photocopies should be declared to the Public Lending Right Authority.

If in doubt, ask. Many authors will allow you to reprint their work for free – but you don't want to be sued, so err on the side of caution every time.

Identify your objectives

Before we leave the subject of *preparation* I need to explain the importance of *objectives*.

You must be crystal clear about the *objective* of your sales letter. Get this straight very early on, while you are still at the preparation stage. What do you want the outcome of your letter to be? What do you want to happen as a result of sending it?

Sometimes you will work on sales letters as a team. Make sure that every team member shares the same *objective*. Thrash this out at the start.

Objectives may not be obvious

A company recently spent £70,000 on their new annual catalogue. Naturally, they wanted a sales letter to accompany the catalogue They showed me the previous year's catalogue at a planning meeting.

'What do you think the *objective* of the letter might be?' I asked.

Not a single person, including the managing director, could tell me.

'To introduce the catalogue,' one person suggested.

'But what is the *objective* of introducing that catalogue with a letter?' I persisted.

The room went quiet. In the end I gave in and told them the answer:

'One *objective* is to make sure as many people as possible become aware that the new catalogue has been published. You also have an *objective* that as many people as possible will read it, and that reading the catalogue will increase sales.'

With the *objectives* established, I was able to work with them. Together we put together a whole campaign and a strategy that would achieve those clear *objectives*.

We decided to run competitions to encourage people to read the catalogue thoroughly. We would offer a free gift to people who managed to find certain specific objects listed in the catalogue.

Simply by running a competition like this, you can quickly find out who in a company is reading your catalogue. You can also find out, potentially, who *hasn't* read the catalogue, and follow that up with a separate telesales campaign or use any other method that appeals to you.

One of our *objectives* was to have people read the new catalogue. This example illustrates clearly why it's so important to know exactly what your letter's *objective* should be.

Residual sales targets

In the health care company I work with we have the objective that our special offer promotional mailings should result in increased residual sales. Let me explain what I mean by the term *residual sales.*

Imagine that you are selling 100 widgets a week. You run a promotion on them for a month, offering a *buy-one-get-one-free* deal. The *objective* of the promotion is to increase the *residual sales* figure.

After the campaign has ended, you establish that your normal weekly sales figure for widgets has settled down to a new level of, say, 120 widgets per week.

That's when you know that your promotion has been a success. Its success is proved by the fact that you now have 20 per cent more people buying the same thing, and paying the full price for it, than you had before.

This increase in sales doesn't just happen for a few weeks – it keeps on happening, indefinitely. *Residual sales* have increased by 20 per cent. Well done.

As you can see, the special offer is used to encourage your customers and prospects to try something that they haven't been trying before.

By being persuaded to try it through a discount or deal, they become exposed to that product. They learn that it's good, it represents value and it provides proper benefits. At this point the product takes on a certain *stickiness*.

Briefly, this means that when a proportion of the people who have tried a new product – because, in part, they were motivated by a discount or greed – continue to buy it afterwards, I describe it as having become *sticky*.

I have learned the hard way that unless your products or services are genuinely good, then the process does not work. A substandard or merely average product will never become *sticky*. People may snap up quantities of your product because you are offering them a great deal – but when the offer ends, they don't buy it any more.

Analyse your promotions carefully. Calculate at what point in the future you will break even, or get your money back on the investment in the promotion. Sometimes your break-even will be an amount of money, but it can also be a time line.

CHAPTER EIGHT
■ Ready to write

THIS SECTION INCLUDES:

- Tone and language
- Offer solutions
- The proposition
- Offers
- Do your sums
- Deadlines
- Scarcity
- Middlemen
- Attention grabbers
- Know your customers

Set the tone

Now that you know who your typical recipient is going to be, and you are clear about your objectives, the first thing to decide is the *tone* of your sales letter.

To use an analogy I find helpful – do you want your letter to read like an article in *The Daily Mirror* or *The Daily Telegraph*? Should the tone be like *The Sunday Sport* or *The News of the World*?

One way to decide on your desired tone is to think about what sort of newspapers your target audience would typically read – and imitate that tone.

Go out and buy that newspaper. Take a look at the writing style. Look at the length of the sentences and the size of the paragraphs. Notice whether they use long words or short words. Work out whether the tone makes you think that you are being spoken to at a board meeting, at a family meal, or at the pub with your mates.

Language

Your objective here is to assume a tone that will create rapport with your readers. You need to be on the same wavelength as your readers. If you can't talk to the people in a language they will understand and respond to, you can never hope to attract their attention.

Try not to use complex words. Never use a big word when a little one – or a collection of little ones – will do. To my mind, *erudite people employ complex words and phraseology so as to exalt themselves.* Not only is this type of phraseology pretentious – it also makes terrible sales copy.

Stick to the KISS method of writing – Keep it Simple, Stupid. Baffling the reader will not win you clients. It just makes it harder to sell anything.

Another tip is to write as if you were writing to your best friend.

Sales copy allows you to break certain grammar rules, even those we had drummed into us at school. Good copy sounds and feels like conversation, not so much like the written word. Good copy is never patronising. It needs to be infused with your enthusiasm and exuberance.

How can you expect your reader to get excited about the sales proposition you're making, if you aren't excited about it yourself? Excitement and enthusiasm are contagious, so make sure your copy is worth catching.

Even if you are not a great copywriter, just write simply, stick with clear, specific and bold messages, and you will not go far wrong.

- Use short words
- Don't patronise
- Don't try to be clever
- Make your copy sound like conversation
- Make your enthusiasm infectious

NEVER AIM TO IMPRESS WITH YOUR VOCABULARY

Problem solving

Let's return to your new video recorder for a moment.

The new machine would solve the problem of your being away a lot mid-week on business. There are some good television programmes on during the week and because you're away you keep missing them. In your frame of reference, missing those programmes is a *problem.*

Yet I have a client who runs an electronics company and has the perfect *solution* to your problem.

Thinking about problems – even apparently simple ones like this – can help you to write truly great copy. Make a list of problems your customers are likely to have. You can even phone them up, as part of your research, and ask them what their biggest daily frustrations are. That's a great question to ask, actually. You'll be amazed at the insight you get into the lives of your customers when you ask that question.

A chance discovery can hold the key

The other evening I was with a highly reputed health care practitioner named Peter Sadler. He told me he had a problem with what he calls DNAs. That day he'd had six DNAs. People who Do Not Appear. Infuriating isn't it? Peter had allocated time and made appointments for those people, yet they did not show up.

Peter could have given those missed appointments to other people waiting for a chance to see him, and who would have turned up. He was understandably agitated.

Now, we probably don't have answers to all Peter's problems. But we can still turn his problems into our opportunities.

We could write to Peter and empathise with him. We could tell him that we know how infuriating it can be, for healthcare practitioners to schedule appointments with people who don't show up. Tell him we know what it's like for the busy practitioner, who has little free time and a tight schedule.

By showing you care and understand, you instantly establish rapport. This is vital for successful sales letters.

Let's imagine we were in a position to sell a health care practice management course. Or we could supply virtual assistants, who could telephone all patients in advance to check they were still able to come. Either of those would enable us to turn Peter's problem to our business advantage.

We would say in our letter that we understand the DNA problem and that we have a solution that may ease the situation.

Never forget the 'what's in it for me?' question for your customers. The reasons your product or service can be useful to them should always be in the front of your mind.

Two magic words

While you are writing your sales letters, or in conversation with a potential client, you need to be aware of 'what's in it for me?' and two other little words that pack a big punch:

SO WHAT?

Let's imagine the electronics salesman is still trying to sell a video recorder to your mother.

'It has a long play feature,' says the salesman proudly.

'So what?' replies your mother (in your imagination).

If he is smart, the salesman will use his creative faculty to come up with a scenario your mother can relate to, and show how the long play feature will solve that problem for her.

When you tell a client about a feature, and he or she says: *'so what?'* this is your cue to articulate the benefit of that feature.

While you are writing your sales letters, you have to imagine a critic is looking over your shoulder and whispering: 'so what?' in your ear all the time.

'So ... that means you only need to put one tape in before you go on holiday for a fortnight, and it can record all your favourite soaps while you're away,' explains the salesman, beaming. Sold.

Anyone who has worked for me as a copywriter will confirm that I often send their work back to them when they list features rather than *benefits.*

Your proposition

You could send out a dreadful sales letter – and still get some 'response'. Enquiries are usually an encouraging 'response'.

The goal is not, however, *response* – it's response followed by conversion. Those enquiries must be turned into paying customers.

What makes people respond valuably is the *proposition.* Not your special offer, not even your promotion, but the whole shebang, which constitutes your *irresistible offer.*

An irresistible offer can multiply the response to your letter many times over. Almost any sales letter will benefit from the inclusion of a special offer, a promotion, or a special invitation.

Your offer has to look so tempting on paper that the reader feels an urge to rush to the phone, get out his cheque book or credit card out and buy that product.

The proposition is more important than your tone, or your choice of words. It is even more pivotal than the *River of Evidence.*

The customer is interested in one thing above all else: *the deal.* You could scribble the right deal on a plain postcard, send it to a prospective customer, and still get the sale.

Where should you put the deal and the benefits?

Make sure you state your proposition early on in your letter. Let it hit your reader between the eyes.

I usually like to place the proposition in the second paragraph. The headline may seem the obvious place for it, however I know from experience that this is a little *too* obvious, and can cause reader resistance. Suffice to say that I recommend you state your irresistible proposition in, say, the first third of the first page.

A sales letter is your chance to write about the benefits of your product or service. State them in a list, with bullet points if you can. Not only does this make them easy to absorb but it makes your letter look great too.

The benefits need to be early in the letter too – for example, in the second paragraph or preferably somewhere in the first page. Your proposition should tempt the recipient to read as far as the list of benefits. He will start to peruse, consider, examine and think about your benefits.

The proposition is like a fishing lure to bring the reader towards you – and then you can hook him with the list of benefits, and finally reel him in.

To summarise:

- Your proposition should answer at least some of the reader's 'what's in it for me?' questions.
- Assuming you're going out to a fertile list your proposition is the most important part of your sales letter, and it will affect response more than anything else.
- Your proposition should be carefully chosen and crafted to suit your target audience.

Free gifts, offers and incentives

Once, when I was again speaking at Cranfield University, I happened to have my SNATCH file with me. It contained a letter from The Caravan Club of Great Britain. My son Ben and I used to have a trailer tent for camping adventures but my club membership had lapsed long ago, and they were trying to re-recruit me.

They were trying to tempt me back with a free gift. It was a waistcoat, in fluorescent orange, and I was supposed to wear it if my car or caravan broke down.

The Cranfield class thought this offer was hilarious. But was this a good proposition or a bad one? For £28 I could sign up for a year and get a free orange waistcoat to wear when my vehicle broke down. The orange waistcoat was probably worth less than five pounds.

In fact, this could be considered a good proposition. It would appeal strongly to serious caravanners who were safety conscious.

It could also be considered a good proposition because it demonstrated that the Caravan Club cares about its members and wants them to be safe.

However we might just as easily consider it a *bad* proposition because it implies that caravan-owners' vehicles break down. It is exposing a negative aspect of caravanning.

I asked my Cranfield class what *they* would do, if they were writing a sales letter for The Caravan Club and the objective was to persuade previous members to rejoin. One suggested that perhaps they would offer discounts at certain campsites, or a discounted membership fee, instead of an orange waistcoat.

To get this right, the students had to put themselves in the audience's shoes and dream up a deal that would appeal to *a caravanner*. What would incite an ex-member of the Caravan Club to get his credit card out right away, pick up the phone and rejoin?

The ex-member needed to be reminded of the great time he used to have out in the fresh air, visiting sights and making new friends. A successful proposition could be linked with that.

With a membership fee of only £28 there is little budget available for an expensive incentive. I assume The Caravan Club bought a bulk order of jackets at a very low unit cost – yet each jacket has a much higher perceived value. They look like they are worth at least £5.00 and my guess is that they cost the Caravan Club a lot less than £1.00.

The time I was able to spend in discussion with my students at Cranfield that day was invaluable. When I'm talking on this topic I can go into much more detail and involve the audience with exercises. It is only through practise that real understanding can be achieved.

Understand the audience

Let's think about a typical caravanner for a moment. What does he look like? What is he wearing? Does he wear a woolly hat? What kind of car does he drive? Is he a successful business executive, or retired? Is he always male? Do women go caravanning, or is it more appealing to couples and families?

Is caravanning an activity for people who want to save money, or for people who have lots of money? Might caravanners be cautious people, who like to be prepared, and always have spare batteries, water canisters and spark plugs with them?

Think about your caravanner. Bring him or her to life in your mind. You may find this difficult.

Break off for a moment, and think instead about the typical person who lives in a mud hut. You probably found picturing a mud hut dweller much easier than the caravanner exercise. But you could characterise caravanners by sorting them into different types.

There might be 'caravanners with families' and 'caravanners whose children have left home', for example.

In fact, I believe that The Caravan Club of Great Britain is very skilled at its direct marketing. They write great sales copy and send out high quality publications.

And they clearly spend a lot of time researching any proposition they make to their customers.

Whatever you think about the fluorescent orange waistcoat, I'll share with you that I believe it is a great proposition.

Older caravanners will like the idea because they are cautious. Younger caravanners will have been reminded of the relatively low cost, camaraderie and outdoor nature of caravanning. Family caravanners will have been reminded of the relative safety and freedom of the hobby.

In short, this sales letter says: *'Join The Caravan Club and if you respond before the end of the month we will send you a waistcoat for you to use in case of a breakdown. It is worth £4.95 and it's yours absolutely free if you book now.'*

Imagine sending a letter with no proposition: it is clear which letter will be the more successful.

The most fascinating aspect of this waistcoat offer is that the Caravan Club has got inside of the minds of their customers and picked exactly the right item for them. Giving discounts can be just too easy: often it is nothing more than giving your money away. There is nothing unique about offering a discount; even to an audience you believe to be cost conscious.

It is likely that the Caravan Club offers a plastic orange jacket to caravan owners because their research shows that this will elicit a greater response than offering a discount. And when you consider that the cost of that jacket was pennies, rather than pounds, it represents a good return on investment.

Everything else you write in your sales letters is there to increase the response to the *proposition*.

Balance the books

When it comes to offers, it is important to get the balance right.

Can you afford to wait 60 days for a response to your offer, or do you want people to respond within three to four weeks? How long would you wait after receiving the membership fees before posting the jackets? Can you afford to order 2,000 jackets – and then only need a hundred? Or will your supplier deliver so quickly, that you have time to order the jackets once you have seen how many you will need?

Most of the big direct mail companies work with companies that specialise in providing incentive gifts. Some incentive suppliers will even fulfil the orders directly with the customer, saving you doing that yourself or contracting a separate mailing house.

Obviously you don't want to end up with a load of unwanted orange jackets. However, business is about taking risks. You may take a leap of faith and invest in 2,000 jackets at 50p each, in order to maximise your returns. Ask yourself whether you can afford the promotion.

Calculate the average cost of a mailing with no colour enclosures. I currently estimate this cost to be about 50p when you include postage, labour and stationery.

When you add a colour printed item to the envelope, the cost goes up to around a pound.

Assume you will send the mailing out to 15,000 people, in a month. The cost of the campaign is now £15,000. Add the cost of the jackets and that's £16,000. As you can see the costs soon add up.

It is a good investment of your time to monitor exactly where your money is going; in relation to the response and returns you receive. Even though it may not be your own personal money, you should have the integrity not to waste company resources on literature that simply does not work.

There are many people in the world of business who are prepared to spend money on ineffective advertising, ineffective copy and ineffective literature. Don't confuse activity with accomplishment. You MUST measure and you MUST test!

Whenever your sales letters fail to attract the desired response, you know it's time to change what you are doing. Keeping an eye on the costs is part of your job.

Measure the effectiveness of previous campaigns and work out how you might logically expect your new one to work.

"Because its purpose is to create a customer,
the business has two – and only two – functions:
Marketing and innovation produce results.
All the rest are costs."
– PETER DRUCKER

Deadlines

An unexpectedly good response to the orange waistcoat offer might mean you run out of gifts before the closing date. In that case, you can write to your customers explaining that they have to wait an extra week or two – owing to the incredible demand you are experiencing after your hugely successful campaign.

Or you might avoid the problem of insufficient incentives by using the words *while stocks last* in your sales letter.

Whatever you do, you must state a deadline in your letter. More than that, restate the deadline two or three times in the letter, especially at the end. Try using words like *'claim yours now'* at the end of the letter. Or use a line such as: *'Stocks allocated to this promotion are limited', so apply before the offer ends on 23rd October 2004 to avoid disappointment.*

The value of scarcity

Scarcity in selling is always effective. Remember that time you were out shopping with a friend, and you both wanted a pair of jeans, but there was only one pair left in the shop? *Scarcity* is a driver.

People buy at times when they wouldn't normally, because of *scarcity.*

A deadline is also a driver that will make people buy at the time of your choosing.

Combine *scarcity* with a *deadline* and you will definitely improve response. Put both elements on a postcard and you'll get a response without the need to write long sentences:

'Here's your special offer. We only have a limited amount, so order now or before we run out on December 31st when the offer closes.'

The intermediate audience, or middleman

What happens when you are writing letters to the middleman, rather than the end user?

For example, you could be selling car radios to car manufacturers. The manufacturer is not the end user but is passing the product on to his own customer. The middleman may not be motivated by price, style or uniqueness; he may be more interested in size or colour or the reliability with which you can deliver.

Your copy needs to emphasise the benefit of the offer for the middleman *and* for his client. Draw the middleman's attention to the fact that if his customer is satisfied it will reflect well on his business and profits.

When dealing with a middleman, you have to bear in mind the 'what's in it for me?' and the 'so what?' questions for the end user as well as the middleman.

Grab the attention

Your sales letters are competing with a huge amount of unsolicited mail from other sources. Many of your readers, like me, probably open and skim read their mail above the bin so that the uninteresting material can drop straight in.

One of the things that will get your mailing piece read and opened, is when you make the right offer, to the right people, written so that they spot it – *before* the bin-reflex has time to strike.

A good offer stops readers in their tracks, while they read and digest your masterpiece. It's a good idea to hint at your incentive in the first or second paragraph – although as a rule of thumb I generally avoid stating the offer as part of the headline although I have to acknowledge that it can work it somehow seems to depersonalise your letter and make it look and feel more like a flyer.

A short line of *teaser* copy, just before and above the headline, can be powerful. For example:

- *'Save £££s this month with this special offer...'*

The headline goes underneath that. Research indicates that a headline can be up to 17 words in length.

There are times when making an offer might *not* be appropriate – but in my experience these occasions are extremely rare. One occasion might be where the brand or the company is so upmarket that making such offers would cheapen and damage the brand.

You would be astonished to know just whose heads are turned by the promise of something free or something extra. Almost anyone can be seduced by the promise of something for nothing. Indeed the proliferation of *buy one, get one free* and other offers we see these days shows that even Tesco, Safeway, Marks & Spencer and others are now actively using this basic approach.

It's hardly surprising that the most powerful word in sales copywriting is the word *free.*

Using the word *free* near the start of the letter – in bold typeface but not in capitals – is almost certain to grab the reader's attention and draw him into reading your letter. Take care however not to over-use it.

Know your customers

To become even halfway competent at writing sales letters, or at any other type of selling, you need to learn to develop profound empathy with your customers. By *profound empathy* I mean the ability to stand in their shoes and think as they do.

Of course this advice applies to the writing of the whole sales letter – but it applies even more to the careful process of designing the perfect proposition for your target audience.

One very important question is:

'Who you are going to send your letter to?'

The answer is:

Your mailing list.

See Chapter Three for more about selecting a mailing list.

Once you have selected your mailing list, it will help you determine the best proposition and offer for that target audience. What you are ideally looking for is people who are genuinely predisposed to your product and services.

Before you start writing, it pays to do some research and discover as much as you can about them. Things you are looking for include average age, likely gender, income bracket, general types of housing they live in, and especially their buying habits.

It is useful to contemplate the old adage: *He could sell fridges to Eskimos.* There is, in reality, not much chance of anyone consistently selling fridges to Eskimos. On the other hand, if you have a special type of stove and heater that runs on fish oil rather than electricity or gas, then that product would undoubtedly be of keen interest to the Eskimo market.

Let's return to my Cranfield students, scratching their heads about the Caravan Club promotion.

You will remember that the mailing's objective was to re-recruit caravanners whose membership of the Club had lapsed. As an incentive for rejoining before a specified cut-off date, it offered a fluorescent orange waistcoat. The waistcoat could be worn by the lucky recipient in the event of a breakdown, thereby increasing his or her safety.

Some students felt the waistcoat offer could have been improved by a simple 50 per cent discount off the first year for re-joining. I pointed out that, as rejoining cost £28, this would have cost the Club £14. I estimated that the waistcoats probably cost the club less than £1 and would probably pull a greater response than an unimaginative discount.

The Caravan Club of Great Britain understands the minds and outlook of most of their members and ex-members. They are good at direct marketing.

There is no doubt that the waistcoat had been a carefully selected enticement to encourage past members to return. I would bet that the waistcoat offer proved a highly successful initiative, as it would probably appeal to their specific target market.

"Before you can inspire with emotion, you must be swamped with it yourself. Before you can move their tears, your own must flow. To convince them, you must yourself believe."
– WINSTON CHURCHILL

Does your product have a theme?

The lesson here should be obvious by now: you must offer the right thing to the right people in order to maximise your results. Even if *the right thing* is not to your personal taste.

For this reason, you should spend time carefully considering your proposition for your target market. Dream up offers in the theme of your products and services.

One additional advantage of *themeing* offers in this way is that you should eliminate many bargain hunters – people who chase the offer merely to claim the free gift but who won't buy from you again unless you offer a similar *bribe*.

Ask yourself: *what is the proposition?*
What is the most important component in my letter?
Which element of this letter is my advertisement?

Special offer gambits in your letters should not be confused with your overall business proposition. This is the element of your business or product that is unique. It is often described as the Unique Selling Proposition (USP). You and your colleagues need to understand fully what it is that is special about your company and what it is that you do that your competitors don't. Ask yourself what you are using as your unique selling point, and make sure you put it across clearly in your letter.

A USP could be:

'The Health Co:Supplying effective nutritional supplements with exceptional customer care and service to health care practitioners.

Another USP could be:

'We sell environmentally sound, safe children's toys made only from renewable resources, to pre-schools and care centres.'

"The BIGGEST mistake I see in marketing
is businesses viewing marketing as an overhead.
It is not an overhead it is an investment.
Good marketing is a good investment which
means you get back more than you put in."
– GARY COURTENAY

CHAPTER NINE
Putting it all together

THIS SECTION INCLUDES:

- Clearing your head
- Understanding AIDA
- Two ready-made systems to simplify the process
- Clearing your head

In this book I have shared an enormous amount of information and advice with you. Your head may well be spinning with benefits, priorities, propositions and objectives. A way of organising this knowledge into a plan would be useful.

Even when you are writing sales letters regularly, you will need a set of procedures to help you to get persuasive copy onto your page. I cannot show you one perfect system that works for everyone – because there is no single perfect system. Everyone has to develop his or her own.

But once you have found the system that works for *you,* applying its rules will get you there, every time. You can start by looking at systems that work for other people, and adapting them to your own needs and personal style.

Let me share *my* system with you first. These are the steps I go through, every time I sit down to write a sales letter:

1. Decide on the objective.
2. Identify features and benefits (sometimes by brainstorming with others).
3. Identify the difference between features and benefits.
4. Dream up the proposition ('create an irresistible offer').
5. Decide on the content.
6. Fish for material from the River of Evidence.
7. Select the facts, figures, statistics and intriguing information I will use.

Understanding AIDA

There is another system, which you may find a useful starting point in developing your own. It may be old but it works extremely well which is why it's stood the test of time.

The system is known as AIDA. The acronym stands for:

- Attention
- Interest
- Desire
- Action

Make sure that the structure and content of your sales letters – and all of your other promotions – follow the AIDA formula, and you will have a winner.

First, get the reader's ATTENTION

You have to hook on to his mind and reel him in. Usually your headline is the chief attention-getter.

Then, arouse their INTEREST

Show the reader that what you have to offer is something he wants.

Now, create a DESIRE

To persuade a reader to part with some cash, you have to stimulate his heart and mind to want what you're offering. Use the third part of your letter to create that *desire* and show the evidence that he really will receive the benefits you've described if he buys.

Finally, ACTION!

In the end, you have to tell the reader, in your simplest words, exactly what you want him or her to *do*. Be very clear and specific. Imagine you are talking to a 12 or 13 year-old. Words of one syllable. Words like: *'Phone 0800 123 4567. Call us now. Don't delay. Buy it now.'*

Now, I know this seems simplistic, even pedantic – but experts have endlessly tested the effect of the *call to action*. I have tested it myself; using newspaper advertisements, and I learned the hard way that if you *don't* call upon readers to take IMMEDIATE action, then they don't and nobody orders.

People hate making their minds up. They hate having to make decisions. Give them a chance to wait for a while, and they will take it – and then forget about it. Success lies in encouraging the reader to make an impulse buy. Research I undertook recently with a group of salesmen showed that only 5 per cent of prospects that said they wanted time to think about it actually converted to customers in the end.

Fail to pounce on the exact moment when that impulse occurs, and your opportunity is lost. Use words like *act now* or *do it now* and *don't wait* and for goodness sake remember to include those two action inducers: 'scarcity' and a deadline/cut off date.

You won't regret it.

"If your actions inspire others to dream more,
learn more, do more and become more,
you are a leader."
– JOHN QUINCY ADAMS

CHAPTER TEN
■ Writing strategy

THIS SECTION INCLUDES:

- Two types of reader
- Principles of good writing
- Tone
- Show interest and understanding
- Powerful key words
- Reading aloud

Principles of good writing

Once you are confident about the practical aspects of your sales letters – the objective, the reader, the content – you can start to refine *how* you write to them.

I mentioned earlier that you need to write in a style which appeals to your readers. It is worth repeating that long words in a sales letter impress nobody. Do not try to come across as an intellectual – it will do nothing to increase your response in fact it will do the exact opposite.

When people skim through a letter, they want to be able to pick up the important points easily. Using simple words increases understanding and response.

The two types of reader

When it comes to the way people read sales letters, there are two basic patterns of behaviour. The first type is the *skim reader.*

He will whiz through your letter, trying to work out what it's about – without reading it all. It is for this reason that your headline, PS, signature, sub-heading, pictures and graphics should conspire to tell him a story and give him the main proposition of your letter.

The other type is the *analytical reader.*

He wants to see facts, figures, statistics and diagrams. If he decides to read, then he will read it all – material from *The River of Evidence* is ideal for him.

Reading it all is also the key characteristic of almost everyone who decides to buy. Sooner or later, most buyers will eventually sit down and read through all of the copy, sometimes more than once.

In a way, you are writing one letter for both types of reader at the same time: the *skim reader* who won't read it all until his swift evaluation is satisfied; and the *analytical reader* who could well have been hooked by the compelling headline alone.

Your letter should be written to satisfy both types – and it's impossible to do this with very short copy.

Many writers never feel comfortable about exceeding one page in length in a business letter. This is because they have forgotten that a business letter is not technically a *sales letter.* A business letter may be your bank statement or a perhaps a letter from your solicitor asking you to come in to his office for a meeting – in other words, they are *letters of information.*

A sales letter aims to be a *letter of persuasion.*

It takes about 30 seconds to read a page of A4. Yet many people believe that in a few seconds they can say enough to convince a prospect to buy whatever it is they're offering.

Imagine standing a real life salesman in front of someone for 30 seconds. It is highly unlikely that he could close a sale for his product or service either.

In reality, your letter must be as long as it needs to be to make the sale. But not a word or even a full stop longer.

Having said that, you should read your draft to eliminate the *yawn factor*. Not everybody could stand up in front of people and talk for a few minutes, completely holding their attention. Yet we often assume that our sales letter will do exactly that.

If you are really concerned that a letter is getting too long, enlist help to reduce the length. When this happens, I usually invite one or two people to read my first draft. They have to be people whose opinions I trust and whose feedback I value. Too many, however, and I find their conflicting opinions tend to confuse more than they clarify.

Keep the tone personal

A letter is the most personal communication that you can give to another person – apart from a kiss. Anyone who has had to write a letter of apology knows how true this is.

A sales letter can transcend all other methods of communication. A successful sales letter should feel *personal*. The recipient should feel as if the letter has been written to him or her alone – not part of a mass mailing.

When you are copy writing, avoid using 'me' words – words such as 'us', 'we', 'our', and your company name. Also avoid impersonal nouns like 'reader' and 'customer' – they are almost guaranteed to reduce response. Instead, whenever possible, replace them with 'you' and 'yours'.

Don't say:
'I'm delighted to tell you that we have a new product which we know will be very popular.'

Instead say:
'You will be delighted to discover a new product is available now – designed specifically to help you grow your business.'

You must understand the difference between these two versions. Even in conversation, we tend to switch off when the other person goes on about 'me, me, me'. People prefer it when you talk about them, ask them questions, and use the word 'you'.

I'll say it again in case you missed it:

PEOPLE SWITCH OFF WHEN YOU TALK ABOUT YOURSELF

Show interest and understanding

Imagine you and I are having a chat. I would talk lots about you and ask questions about you and your life; you would like that. And if I were to talk about you and your problem with patients who don't turn up – your DNAs – suddenly you would be even more interested.

Now picture your letter in your customer's hand. It is full of excitement about the tenth anniversary of your company. The customer is skim reading – and walking towards the bin. Every time he reads one of your 'me' words, he goes six inches closer to the bin. Every time he reads a 'you' word he moves six inches away from it. Too many 'me' words and your letter is *in* the bin.

Without wishing to sound brutal, he is not interested in knowing about your company's anniversary or that you have just served your millionth customer.

All he wants to know is that you've got something he can make money from, or that you can help him with his business problems or even more simply, you have something for him from which he can benefit. Your company's anniversary is of no interest to him.

The words you choose will transform the quality of your copy.

A rule of thumb is:

For every 'ME' use five 'YOUs'.

Here's a great test to conduct on each and every letter before it goes out the door. Go through your copy with two highlighter pens, highlighting all the 'MEs' in one colour and the 'YOUs' in another. The correct balance will quickly become obvious.

Powerful key words

Here is a selection of key phrases I use with promotions and letters, all of them tested for effectiveness. They will transform your copy:

- Free, save, pay nothing, performance guaranteed, money back if not delighted – announcing, secrets, breakthrough
- Act now, call us now, amazing, at last
- Deadline, the closing date is XX, until stocks expire, cut off date, discover
- Don't be disappointed, order yours now, limited stocks have been allocated, new, sale, bargains, protect, hate
- Here's how you will benefit, this is what you can expect, how to
- Don't miss out, call us now to be sure of yours, last time we ran this we sold out in…
- We've saved one for you for 7 days, there are not enough to go round, how would, the truth of, protect

Whenever you spot other good phrases and devices, in other people's sales material, add them to the list.

Once you have your *River of Evidence* material and your lists of keywords and phrases you will find that 80 per cent of your letter has virtually written itself.

Even if you don't consider yourself a writer, you will get results this way. Those results will pay you massive dividends.

Read aloud

It is a good idea to compose your letter in longhand. You need to be at your most creative for this job, and handwriting uses and stimulates the right-hand, creative, side of the brain.

Once you have drafted the letter, read it back to yourself. Read it out loud.

Reading aloud triggers your subconscious so that you become more aware of the structure of the words. Many phrases that look fine on the page sound completely wrong when read aloud. Great copy reads beautifully when you read it aloud.

Having read it aloud, rewrite it. Yes you did read that correctly. Turn away from your first draft and write it again. By doing this you will often find yourself latching on to a fresher, better way of saying the same thing second time around.

Of course, in my consultancy work, I have to read a lot of sales letters so that I can write the best, most powerful, copy for my clients.

Read excellent sales copy letters, written by other people. Read them aloud. Rewrite *them* in your own words. And if you are really keen to learn then re-write them in longhand. This is a powerful exercise. I know this because I read a lot of sales copy and sometimes find myself rewriting other people's words in my own letters. I'm never quite sure where some of the phrases I use come from – I believe the reason I have retained them is because I knew instinctively that they were compelling when I first read them.

Create empathy

One thing that turns an ordinary writer into a great sales copywriter is *empathy*.

This quality enables you to understand how your target audience is feeling, and to share their feelings.

Before you read on you should ask yourself whether you really know what empathy means. In one of the other workshops that I deliver, I ask everybody present to give me their version of the word *empathy*. Incredibly out of a room of, say, 15 people, I might find just one or two who fully understand the meaning of the word. Most of the replies I get are more akin to the word *sympathy*.

It is not the same as *sympathy*, which means you feel sorry for someone. Empathy is the ability to put yourself in the shoes of others, and to see an issue from their perspective.

If there is one paramount thing I do, which enables me to write words that get people reaching for their cheque books, credit cards and even their cash, it is that I try to see things from their point of view. I powerfully determine who my most typical recipient will be and then I imagine what it's like to be him or her. I imagine what it's like to live their lives and deal with the same daily triumphs and disasters that they do. And there is no doubt that I am good at feeling empathy. Why though? I'll tell you why. Because I realise that the ability to feel massive empathy with your target audience is essential to good sales copy writing. I have worked hard at developing empathy as a core skill.

How can you highlight the benefits that will be key to your prospect unless you understand firstly what it is that is of value to them?

For some people, empathy is instinctive. To become a great copywriter you must become empathetic, whether or not it comes to you naturally. This is how you can talk about the reader's problems, tug at his heartstrings, and create the kind of rapport that makes him feel he is special to you.

CHAPTER ELEVEN
Refine your writing style

THIS SECTION INCLUDES:

- Structure and layout
- Headlines, paragraphs and sub-headings
- The signature
- Bullet points
- Fonts
- Call to action
- PS
- Long or short?

Structure and layout

Certain things belong in specific places in a sales letter. Although some of this may seem obvious, it is worth taking the time to understand *why* those elements have been found to work best in those places.

We also need to consider the impact of sub-headings, signature, style, ink, colour, bullet points and so on. Use each of these elements properly and you will increase response. Miss one out and you will actively decrease response.

Headlines, paragraphs and sub-headings

In order to illustrate the power of headlines, appropriate phrasing and so on, I am now going to tell you a true story about one of my earliest forays into sales copywriting. When I was studying management at Manchester Polytechnic, I used to come home every summer, broke.

Like all students, my friends and I did odd jobs – working in bars, washing dishes, collecting glasses and so on. Fed up with this, my pal Denton and I decided to try something different, hoping to do better financially.

We asked ourselves what skills we had. For a start, we could certainly do what we'd always done at home for our parents. Two strapping lads like us could probably handle a spot of gardening in exchange for payment.

A business was born

Despite knowing very little about the subject, we put an advertisement in *The Blackpool Evening Gazette.* We combined our names – Denton and Courtenay – and thus our business was born.

We won two out of every five enquiries

Each time we placed our ad, we would typically receive five enquiries. We would visit each prospect, and give them estimates for the work they wanted. From these we would usually win at least two gardening projects.

In our ad we described Dencourt Garden Services as *the customer's choice for flagging, concreting, turfing, fencing, garden clearance* – and anything else we thought we could tackle.

By taking on any reasonable sounding project, we were making more money then we had ever experienced in our lives. The pubs and discos of Blackpool became our playground every weekend. After grafting in other people's gardens all week we would cheerfully blow everything we'd made, ready to start all over again on Monday.

We cleared gardens and laid paving stones, concreted paths and bases for sheds as well as laying the turf. In fact we would have a go at just about anything. Consequently, we earned more money than we had ever earned in our lives. It was amazing.

Encouraged by this success, we put the advert in every week. More clients responded, we did more gardening, and our earnings soared.

Then I got smart. I began to wonder what might happen if I messed about with the advert. I played and tinkered with the original wording.

Now the original advert had a structure similar to this but of course these were not the exact words:

'We do gardening and here is a list of the things we do. Phone this number for a free quotation.'

This time I just changed the first three words of the advert and found that we got around six times the response. We received between 30 and 40 phone calls over the weekend that the new ad appeared. So much work came in that we spent the following week doing nothing but estimates.

What made the difference was the words – just three words had been changed in the advert. Keep reading and I'll let you know what they were a little later in this chapter . . .

We looked at each other in astonishment. The new ad, costing exactly the same as the old one, brought six times the response. Denton and I looked at each other in astonishment.

Our prices went up and we became more selective

We spent the first week doing nothing but quotations – and wondered whether the new ad had backfired on us! However we soon realised that we had more work than we could cope with. Our response was to put our prices up and we became more selective about the jobs we took on. Now we could afford to choose only the easiest and the most profitable.

We were turning business on and off like a tap

Our earning power doubled. We also reduced our biggest overhead – the cost of advertising. Now we only needed to advertise occasionally, and we could control the flow of new business, turning it on and off like a tap.

How did we do it?

This transformation in our fortunes was down to three little words. The main thing I fiddled with in our ad was the first three words, which would always appear in bold. They now said: TRY MY PRICES. The rest of the copy rattled off the list of jobs we could do – exactly as we had always done in the previous ads.

This was my first lesson in the power of headlines.

TRY MY PRICES

It was just a classified advert

When we think of headlines we usually think of bold writing in much bigger size than the text it sits above. In the case of Dencourt Gardeners, it was just a classified advert in a standard column, and only those first three *magic* words were in bold.

Imagine the impact those few words made on our business! We were only 18 and had no intention of building a business. We were due to go back to college soon. All we wanted was to make money so we could afford to go to the pub and enjoy ourselves.

In the end, we generated more work than we could cope with. At that point we could afford to be selective about which clients we took on. In the beginning we had taken on anything we could get.

With this new oversupply of work we put our prices up. We would do only the jobs we wanted to do, that were closest to our homes, that made us the most profit, and that were for people we liked.

At 18 years old, Denton and I learned a valuable lesson: marketing is powerful stuff. Get the words right in your advert, and you can improve the quality of your life by giving yourself more choices. When you have more work than you can cope with, you can feel reassured that you are passing the least profitable and most awkward jobs with the meanest clients on to your competitors.

GET THE WORDS RIGHT

The headline can make your sales letter – or break it

Thirty years have passed. Many times since then, I have seen that same phenomenon of headlines work in a similar way and massively multiply results.

A headline can make or break your advertisement or sales letter. After the *proposition*, it is the most important element.

Good headlines multiply response for free. Thousands of case studies show how advertisements have increased their response by ten fold or even more – by replacing a weak headline with a good one. The copy beneath it remained unchanged. There was no additional marketing cost.

Whatever happened to the Dencourt lads?

Just for the record, Dencourt carried on for the next three years as a highly successful and lucrative part time business.

Still in my early twenties and with college behind me I left Dencourt to my business partner, Denton, and used the money I had eventually saved to travel abroad for several years, seeking fame and fortune.

Some great headlines

- *At sixty miles per hour the loudest noise in the Rolls Royce was the ticking of the clock*

What a headline. It tempts you to read the rest of the article.

- *Do you make these mistakes in English?*

This headline was used in American newspaper advertisements for forty years and was hugely successful – if a little strange.

One particular American Express sales letter is generally deemed one of the most successful sales letters of all time. It began like this:

- *Yes, it's true, the American Express Card isn't for everyone . . .*

While these words appeared in the first paragraph of the letter, and the letter itself had no headline, they still count as the headline as they are the first words the reader sees. The letter continued rather like this:

- *Dear Mrs Jones*

  Quite frankly, The American Express Card isn't for everyone and not everyone who applies for card membership is approved.

That choice of words was so effective that American Express found they could not afford to drop it, even after extensive testing of other wording. They simply could not find anything else that recruited customers as well as that letter – and those words weren't even in the headline. They were the opening sentence.

Hundreds of the world's millionaires attribute at least some of their success to my colleague, American marketing guru Jay Abraham. Jay is best known in this country for his three-day marketing seminars of which I am occasionally the MC. Incidentally, they cost around £3,000 to attend. He often uses direct mail to promote them and one particular headline springs to mind whenever I think of Jay, because he uses it so often and it seems to work every time:

- *I have just got to get this off my chest before it explodes.*

You can use this headline for almost anything. Jay has sent me so many examples of this headline in use and yet, even though I'm familiar with it, it is so powerful that it compels me to read on. Somehow even though I know the headline it still tricks me to read on. That headline just works.

The headline is there to draw the reader in. To attract the reader's attention. Immediately. To hook him, and compel him to read on. It takes less than three seconds for the reader to decide whether to read on or bin a letter, as I have said before.

A headline sets out your stall. It may be a synopsis of what follows in the main body of the letter, in which case it works like a *teaser*. Whatever, it tempts you to read on.

Whether your headline is for a newspaper article, an advertisement, or a sales letter, its reason for being there is the same. If your material has no headline, the same applies to the first few words of the text – the opening words become a substitute headline.

Newspapers are so sure that headlines are powerful things that they employ sub-editors to write them. Journalists write the articles but it is sub-editors who write the headlines. Being a headline writer demands tremendous skill.

Headlines are worth the effort

Never be in any doubt that some of the response generated by your sales letters will be determined by how good, or bad your headline is. This is why the big users of direct mail, such as Readers Digest, continually test one headline against another to see which ones pull the best.

If the job of writing headlines is going to be your responsibility, prepare to spend as much time writing them as you spend on writing the letter itself. You can buy books of headlines, or even *borrow* headlines from history. The book *Words That Sell* by Richard Bayan is packed with useful words, phrases and tried-and-tested headlines.

It is not enough to write down ten different headlines and then sit back. You need more than that – maybe 20, maybe more. Once you have written about 20 headlines, *then* you can pick the best one.

But I warn you, often the headline you like *least* will surprise you in tests and can outperform your favourites – sometimes by a huge margin. It is worth putting your headlines to a vote. Find out what other people think of them. Create a *committee* if you can to help you select your headlines. You may find that everyone picks the headline you like least.

The truth is, you can never be sure how your target audience is going to respond to a headline. Many marketers come unstuck, and entrepreneurs go bust, because they believe they *know* their customers and they second-guess what they want. This is especially true of entrepreneurs who believe they are skilled marketers but go on to prove they are not.

It is fair to say that most entrepreneurs have some kind of a flair for marketing – but ironically, only the tiniest proportion have ever taken any training in the subject.

As is always the case in marketing, my opinions, yours and even those of a whole group of your colleagues are of little importance. When you test you give your personal market the opportunity to vote about what they like and what they don't like. They will vote with their orders and if you test properly you can easily see which of your marketing materials and ideas are the ones that provide the best response. It is the foolish man who, even after years of experience, thinks he can select the best performing headline from a list of many.

This applies to numerous other component parts of your mailing too.

In the health care business I work with we have a product that we promote annually and on which we would do a *buy one get one free* offer. Imagine our surprise when we tried *buy five and get the sixth one free* and it way out-pulled the previous offer.

Below is a list of some of the most influential elements of your mailing that you can test against each other.

- The list – the people you mail out to
- The proposition/special offer
- The headline
- Envelopes
- Copy length – make it longer/shorter and see what happens
- The signatory
- Enclosures (perhaps from the River of Evidence)
- Personalisation (Dear Mr Johnson) against Dear Colleague etc

You would do well to type up the words that follow and stick them up somewhere in your office lest you ever forget them:

"At the end of the day it is people who buy from you that are your judge, your jury and even your executioner."

Regardless of whatever you and any panel of so-called experts may think, it is the people who buy from you who will decide if your latest offering is successful or not. So give them the chance to tell you what they think by voting with their orders.

Paragraphs and sub-headings

The purpose of a headline is to lead you to read the whole letter.

Paragraphs with sub-headings above them encourage the reader to read *just one paragraph* – and then to become so involved that he keeps reading the next paragraph, and the next, until the end.

Keep your paragraphs short. Make them interesting enough to keep the reader's attention hooked. Keep whetting his appetite about a revelation to come, and keep him reading until the end when you unveil the deal.

Some of your paragraphs can be as short as a single sentence.

That creates quite an impact and keeps the pace going nicely. If something is really important I often make the point stand alone in its own paragraph.

You must set a 'house style' for paragraph handling, decide once and for all, whether you will indent your paragraphs, use boldface and so on.

Anti-skim reader device

The purpose of a *sub-heading* (or sub-head) is to lead into the following paragraph. A skim reader may flick down the page, taking in nothing but the sub-headings. But a powerful sub-heading will arrest his attention and make him read that paragraph. With sub headings there is then a better chance of a skim reader reading more of your letter.

For inspiration, when you are writing a sub-heading, simply dip into the paragraph that follows – and cut and paste a few words. Select four or five of the most tantalising, taunting words and use them.

- 'Fantastic discounts if you act now'
- 'Apply by 22nd March for this unbeatable free offer'
- 'Gold members enjoy these exclusive benefits and privileges'

To save space, you might choose not to put a line-break between the sub-heading and the paragraph. Let it sit right on top of the paragraph body copy. Then put it in bold type, align it to the centre of the line, and use a capital letter for the first word only. You will see an example of this in the Appendix.

Of course your company style may already favour using no capitals and having sub-headings aligned at the left. As long as you adopt a clear style and stick to it, you will be fine.

Sub-headings are like bookmarks

People often read quickly and superficially – you and I included. We do this because we are pushed for time and need to ascertain whether something is of use to us or not in double quick time. When you are trying to evaluate what's in a document as quickly as possible, you run your eyes over the page and pick out the most important details.

In your sales letters, you will highlight the most important details for the reader as sub-headings.

When you read quickly, your eyes jump from sub-heading to sub-heading. As a copywriter, your job is to make sure that your readers get the most important and relevant information about your proposition, when they are skimming your letter.

Sub-headings are vital to the success of your letter. They need to catch the attention and interest of the reader – who may have already decided he is not interested in your letter even before he starts reading.

Bullets

I love bullet points. But they can be over-used. Fourteen bullet points in a list is far too many – you can tell just by looking at it.

Whenever you find yourself with a long list of bullet point items, go back and put them in order of importance. Then just use the first five or six. More than this spoils the look and often gives an amateur appearance.

The simple rule is too many points looks wrong. Fewer points make an impact.

Perhaps the rejected bullet points in your long list seem too good to waste. In this case, consider using them in another list on the next page.

FEWER POINTS MAKE AN IMPACT

Fonts

Thanks to computers, it is easy to use ten or 20 typefaces in a single document. You have a huge range of point sizes at your fingertips too. And there are special effects such as bold, italic and underline.

Don't do it.

The more you vary the font size and style, the more confusing it is for the reader. Select one typeface, or font, and stick to that. The font called Times New Roman was specially developed to increase comprehension. Consequently, it should come as no surprise that tests have shown Times New Roman generates the best response in sales letters.

These days it has become trendy to use a *sans serif* font, such as Arial. *Sans serif* means a plain font that does not have tails on the characters. This font may perhaps be a reasonable choice, where your business or target audience is trendy too.

Signature

A good signature is the finishing touch to any well-written letter.

In the case of a sales letter, the signature has to look natural and realistic. Although the signature will be printed at the same time as the rest of the letter, there are a few obvious conventions to follow that will help it give your letter a personal and authentic feel.

The signature should be printed in blue, in contrast to the rest of the copy, which will usually be in black. It should look hand written, perhaps as if it has been signed with a ballpoint pen, the commonest implement used for signing letters these days.

Tests have shown that a signature written in a font called *Reflex*, which is blue with a fairly narrow felt tip pen brings the very best response.

Have a look at the signature I use in my own sales letters. It was developed specifically for use in direct mail and is full of devices aimed at creating the right assumptions in the mind of the reader.

In summary: always make sure your signatures are blue and are legible. Make sure that the signatory is the most important person in the company if you can. Your aim should be to create a signature that makes the letter look and feel that it has been created and sent personally to the recipient and not part of a mass mailing. Apply the signature in the wrong way, making it look mass produced and you can give the game away and undo all your hard work.

If nothing else remember this: signatures properly applied increase response.

We make assumptions about people, based on their signature. A small, neat signature would make you think of a meticulous, maybe rather boring, person, while a large signature full of loops and flourishes looks like it comes from a larger than life creative type.

These are just assumptions and whether they are true or not is immaterial. You will probably get the best results if the signature succeeds in making you seem outgoing and energetic.

You will notice that my signature rises upwards to the right. I'm trying to create an impression that I'm heading onwards and upwards – and that the reader could get there with me.

This is certainly contrived. But it works – it increases response.

Just as a point of interest, I will often use a fountain pen to sign individual letters, This looks simply wonderful. You can also get a credible self-inking rubber stamp made of your signature in places such as Office World and these can be handy for short runs of around 50 – 100 when you are not present to sign. A typical short run application would be writing to your key accounts.

Whose signature?

It may be appropriate to sign your own sales letter. If so, make your signature legible and stylish.

I have discovered in most cases that it increases response when the company's CEO signs the letter. It gives a better impression, commands attention and thus increases response.

Customers respect experts and professionals too, so it is a good idea to get your letters signed by someone in the field who has a good reputation and appropriate connectivity with your company. Find someone with a passion for your industry, lots of charisma, and who is happy to help you. You may have to come to some commercial arrangement with them, though.

If you don't have an expert or a CEO to hand, ask yourself who might be the best person, the most influential person or the most important person in your organisation– and ask him or her to sign the letter.

Readers would always prefer to receive a letter from someone important. Creating the illusion that someone eminent has written the letter provides enormous impact and can increase response.

The down side of asking your CEO to sign the letter is that some readers might call him in response to the letter. This is generally undesirable, so make sure the letter directs enquiries to the correct department.

Call to action

You need a *call to action* at the end of every sales letter. It belongs in the very last part of your final paragraph. Always include a cut-off date in your call to action. Let the reader know that stocks are limited if applicable. Make your call to action read rather like an hypnotic command. Make the reader believe that if he does not act now, he could lose out.

Even when you have announced a cut-off date, you may still be prepared to extend it or even order in more stock to fulfill additional orders. You might enclose a voucher that says: *'use within two weeks'* – and that needs a cut-off date too. People can't help being driven by scarcity and deadlines. Or put another way, if you don't give your reader lots of reasons to act immediately then probably they won't.

A great offer and a tight deadline

The other day I went to Marks & Spencer and spent £150. To my astonishment the assistant handed me three £5 gift vouchers, saying: *'Special offer this weekend. For every £50 you spend, you receive a £5 gift voucher.'* At first I was delighted. Then I got thinking.

'Excuse me,' I asked. 'Does this mean that I could bring one of these items back tomorrow, get a refund and then buy it again using my vouchers, so that I get £15 off the item?'

'Ah, but you wouldn't do that, sir, would you?' she said with a wry smile. 'You look far too nice a person.'

Of course I didn't do that. But I *could* have. Instead I went back to M&S that following week – and I didn't just spend the £15 vouchers. I spent another £150. And that's the power of how this type of offer works.

Don't overlook the simple stuff. It works. Every time you spot a good offer that works, ask yourself how you might adapt it to use in your own business. Play with the concepts and ideas that work for others, and challenge yourself to think of ways to incorporate them into your sales campaigns and projects.

PS (Post Script)

The PS is a vital part of your letter and I recommend that you always use one. Research shows that many skim readers will skip through your letter making their way as quickly as they can to the signature to see if it is a) a real signature and b) who has signed it. It's at this point that the PS comes into its own as it sits just below the signature, which accounts for why it is so frequently read. Properly crafted, the PS can contain wording that hooks the skim reader into reading the entire letter. Even if the letter is read conventionally special attention is given by the reader to the PS. So the PS gives you a wonderful opportunity to have the last word. Don't waste it. Use it to reinforce one of your main points or simply let it be a short summary of your entire letter.

Sometimes you have to break a rule, and this is true when you consider the use of fonts in a PS.

I always change to a different font for the PS. I switch to the font called Courier. The idea is that this makes the text look as if it has been typed on an old fashioned typewriter.

Before computers became commonplace that is exactly how PS's were often produced. The secretary would take the newly typed letters to the boss for signing – and the boss would suddenly think of something else to add to the letter. And he would want it to be typed on afterwards.

Research by people like Readers Digest shows that a PS in Courier will bring a greater response than a PS in the same font as the rest of the letter such as Times New Roman.

Another trick to make the PS really effective is to get it hand written for real.

Ask someone with really nice handwriting to write out the PS in block capitals, in blue ink. There are fonts that imitate various styles of handwriting but for a PS you can't beat the real thing. A handwritten PS lends credibility to the idea that the letter has been written to each reader individually. Most readers will suspect it's not a one-off letter at all. But the trick is to provide them with no evidence that it is part of a mass mailing and confirm their suspicions.

In short, make sure your PS looks different from the rest of your letter.

If the letter is printed in bold, write the PS in plain. Making them different gets extra attention.

The PS must contain a special message. Don't waste it. Get this right and it will have a positive effect on your response.

You may not be sure what to include in the PS. In this case, make it a short summary of the content of the letter. Perhaps you could remind the reader not to forget to claim his special offer and of the closing date of your promotional deal. Or you could use it to repeat in different words the key benefit of your product or service. There are no hard and fast rules for a PS. The main thing is that you use yours to create content that will help to increase response to your letter.

Alternatively you can use your PS to introduce something completely new. For example, you could advise the reader about a special promotion he will hear about next month. You can even *fanfare* this offer further by saying, for example, that only a small number of products will be available so to look out for a pink envelope in your post. You could perhaps use the PS for a forthcoming event you want to promote, if you wanted. The possibilities are endless.

Length

I used to believe that the perfect length for a sales letter was one page.

It is true that an American *resumé* has to fit on one page, and that a cover letter supporting an application should be one page long. British *curriculum vitae* can be up to three pages, but the cover letter must still be a single page.

I have learned to accept that it's a good idea in most cases to keep a business letter down to one page in length. However I have written countless letters that ran over to more than one page, and I don't worry when they do. No harm will come to you if you break the one-page rule.

When we are selling face-to-face to somebody, we can see how well our presentation is going, estimate the customer's response, and adjust our approach accordingly. When all we have is the written word, we start at a disadvantage.

To get around this disadvantage, as sales copywriters we have to know our subject inside out: the product or service, and our prospective customer. Our sales copy should answer and deal with all of the most common objections that might arise if the prospect were stood in front of us and possibly some of the less common objections too.

This is the approach I recommend that you take when you write sales letters. But it is almost impossible to write a properly persuasive letter in one page.

Your letter should be punchy and to the point. It will be improved by including interesting information that is genuinely valuable and useful to the reader. It is for this reason that you should take the first draft of your long letter and shorten it by eliminating anything that might cause a loss of attention.

Loss of attention is the enemy. Moments after attention is lost, your letter will be consigned to the bin.

LOSS OF ATTENTION IS YOUR ENEMY

Don't take my word for it – read the research

There is fascinating research on business letter length, based on the millions of letters sent out by huge companies. The research proves that long copy *out-pulls* short copy, almost every single time.

Pause for a moment to absorb that astonishing fact. This phenomenon has been tested on millions of recipients, by very large corporations, who take their sales results very seriously. They send out millions of one-page letters, and millions of two-page letters, and measure the variation in response rate.

This is fact, not hearsay. Here is even more evidence.

In his book *How to Write Sales Letters that Sell*, Drayton Bird says: 'In 37 years of writing, I have never known a short letter *making the same proposition* do better than a long letter".

Bird also talks about Richard V Benson, the man many believe to be the outstanding direct mail exponent in America. Benson has created what he calls *Thirty-one Rules of Thumb*. Rule #18 is, quite simply: 'Long copy beats short copy.'

Look at the *junk mail* you receive at home. Notice how much of the mail that goes straight into the bin is just one page long.

One type of business that excels at sending single page letters is the credit card company. I don't even bother to open the envelopes to judge whether they are good enough for my SNATCH folder any more. Perhaps credit card companies simply do not realise how much money they are wasting? They must be making *some* money out of sending those one-page letters – otherwise they wouldn't keep on doing it.

If only someone would tell them how much *more* money they could be making with a longer letter.

When you write your own sales letters, don't obsess about the length before you start. Say everything you need to say. Think of every possible objection or reason that your customer could come up with, even in the back of his mind, for not buying your product or service.

Then make sure you answer all those objections in your copy.

LONG COPY OUT-PULLS SHORT COPY

Write long, cut short

Testing your letters will reveal what works for your business. You may find that when you allow yourself to write a much longer letter, you will inadvertently write much more than you need to. When this happens, the advice is to *write long and cut short.*

When you have finished your letter, discipline yourself to go back through it. Edit it carefully. Cut it back and pare it down. The golden rule in journalism is to cut and cut and cut again. Say everything that you need to say but in as few words as possible.

You will find that when you start cutting your copy, it becomes more compelling and interesting. Tight copy is more likely to keep your reader involved. When you use more words than you need, and you risk *banging on* about your product or service.

There is nothing worse than walking round a car while the salesman talks at you non-stop. You may end up feeling like hitting him over the head with a rolled up brochure just to make him shut up. We have all suffered the attentions of that sort of salesman.

Your copy must be engaging, enchanting and informative. It must be packed with information and value. This is one reason why we can get away with long sales letters. But even though you may take the utmost care with the content of your sales letters, most of them will end up in the bin. Console yourself that in direct mailing the proportion of your effort that doesn't get a response is much larger than the part that does.

Getting your direct mail campaign right can be tough and time consuming and you may be interested to know that I am also involved in a business that offers software solutions for task and project management that transform the way people work. It gives you the ability to manage scores of projects and tasks and makes easy work of handling your direct mail projects too. But if you need to remember one rule above all others it is this:

Quite simply, a sales letter should just be as long as it needs to be, in order to sell the item. And not a word longer.

Ian Ogilvy, one of the giants of the advertising world, said:

"The trouble with advertising is that half of it doesn't work. The trouble is we don't know which half."

Wise words.

CHAPTER TWELVE
Materials

THIS SECTION INCLUDES:

- Paper
- Envelopes
- Lumps
- To brand or not to brand?
- Postcards

The subliminal message

The materials which bring your message to the reader speak volumes at a very deep and sometimes subconscious level. They are as important as the words you use in your mailing.

The texture, weight, smoothness, glossiness, thickness, colour and size of each element can be chosen to enhance the words within.

Paper

The type of paper you use for your letter makes a difference. It sets the tone.

Don't use cheap, light paper, some recipients will probably think that you are cheap and light too. Typical photocopier paper weighs 80 grammes. Whenever possible use something heavier than 80 grammes. Deep down, whether they realise it consciously or not, most people consider 80 gramme paper to be *ordinary*. You do not want to be ordinary. Use 100 gramme, if you can.

Consider using textured paper. Some paper is beautifully embossed, some looks like parchment. Select your paper according to your audience. Yes it can be expensive but if it increases response you should look upon it as a good investment.

For example, if you are selling fine wines by direct mail, you might like to use a good quality parchment paper, printed in burgundy coloured ink. You might even have a photograph or line drawing of a famous chateau in France as part of your logo.

The objective is to achieve a subliminal effect on your reader via your paper and envelopes. Everything makes a difference, and as a general rule of thumb it's worth paying the extra for.

Envelopes

When most people get a sales letter, research shows that they pick it up and look first at the envelope. And it improves response if the envelope appears to be handwritten.

Of course, hand writing thousands of envelopes yourself is impractical. Fortunately there are fonts that simulate handwriting. Nightingale Conant, the world's leading publishers of business and self development material, uses these fonts a lot.

If the envelope is an unusual size and shape, this also helps response. Nightingale Conant is the expert at this. The last envelope I received from Nightingale Conant was bright yellow and A4 in size.

We all receive white A5 envelopes bearing the name of the company trying to sell us a credit card. If you are at all like me, you will put most of these straight in the bin. We both know immediately what the content will be about, so we don't even bother opening them.

Perhaps credit card companies should test leaving the logo off their envelopes. It might increase the chances of the letter being opened, at least. It's impossible to estimate exactly what these card companies spend on such solicitations but I estimate that several million must be wasted each year. Tragically, those wasted letters could have brought a much better response.

When you write direct mail, the biggest possible insult to your work is that your letters go in the bin unopened.

Lumps

Your primary job is to make sure you get your letter opened. One trick is to use 'lumpy mail'. *Lumpy mail* sells.

It works like this: you put a lumpy object in your envelope and it will get opened.

This need not be anything expensive. Even I take the time to extract the cheap ballpoint pens from the envelopes that contain them.

Incredibly there is in fact a company called lumpymail.com that specialises in selling all kinds of *lumps* for your envelopes.

You may recall, from the *River of Evidence* chapter, a mailing containing a packet of porridge in the envelope. We put the letter, the pills and the porridge oats in a big white A4 Jiffy bag. People don't often receive Jiffy bags in the post, and when they do, they usually contain something interesting, like a present. That worked in our favour.

It can be useful to brand the envelope with an element of your corporate identity – for instance your logo or slogan. Assuming your company already has a good reputation, people will open your envelope because they already know and like you.

Branding and teaser copy printed on your envelope can work well, especially when you have a strong pre-existing relationship with the customer. This approach can be useful when writing out to a loyal customer base offering them something new.

When your letters have a reputation for containing useful information, that is another reason why they will be opened. A newsletter, for example, may be very useful to the recipient.

In the case of the health care company I work with, the letters we send out are 95 per cent information, and only five per cent offer.

People open our letters. Some even look forward to receiving them. We tell them about industry news and trends – and why our product is arriving at just the right time.

LUMPY MAIL MAKES PEOPLE CURIOUS

Teasers

Try putting what is known as *teaser copy* on your envelope. This could be as obvious as *fantastic special offer inside.* You might add a little information about your company, if you think that will help.

In a perfect world, I would send out every single sales letter in a plain envelope with a genuinely handwritten address. That ideal envelope would probably be A5 and look as if a friend had sent it. Personally, I cannot resist an envelope from a friend.

Interestingly there are many direct mailers who use students, housewives and others to hand address envelopes. The reason they go to all this trouble and avoidable expense is because it lifts response so much it easily pays for itself.

Rubber stamps

Believe it or not, rubber stamps increase response. Whenever someone sends in an enquiry, always rubber-stamp the envelope you send in response. Your stamp could say something like *'Information you requested enclosed.'* Or you could stamp it with something even simpler: *'URGENT'*.

It is possible to have a fake rubber stamp graphic pre-printed on your envelopes – but the key is to make it look authentically hand stamped.

Coloured envelopes

There is an argument for making some of your envelopes tinted simply because the majority of envelopes are either white or buff. When a customer receives a coloured envelope, they may take it for a greetings card and feel compelled to open it.

Postage stamps

A franked envelope looks as if it has come from a business. With an ordinary postage stamp on your envelope, it looks more like something sent by a friend. Of course using a franking machine is much simpler and quicker, but it signals to the recipient that this is a business letter rather than something personal. Many Post Offices will stick single stamps on your mailing if you give them notice. Sometimes they won't even charge you for it.

Variety

Readers Digest uses a huge variety of envelope sizes and colours. They use a variety of stickers and 'special customer' labels too. They do this because variety increases response.

Try to change the look of your mailings now and again. Change from an A4 envelope to A5. Occasionally, send out a plain envelope, and use a different font for the address. Add an interesting lump from time to time. Become intriguing.

Every time you have a new product, consider sending out a free sample. Invite the recipient to try the product or service for free, and to let you know how they get on. That's a *very* personal message.

This can be especially powerful. Sending larger, more valuable samples to a few key customers can reap dividends. Take it a step further. Invest in hiring someone to telephone all the recipients, asking what they thought of the free sample. Just this tip can repay your investment in this book a thousand fold.

At the start of this book I mention a colleague of mine, Chris Payne. Chris is one of the best sales copywriters in the country, and his company is called Life Tools. His sales letters are fabulous. To see for yourself how they are put together, I recommend that you simply look up his phone number and ask to be included on his mailing list. But be warned, Chris's letters are so compelling you will probably end up buying at least some of the items on offer. To contact Life Tools see the resources section at the back of the book.

Branding

Your corporate identity is important to your business – but how important is it to your sales letter?

Most of the direct mail you receive will contain a letter on headed paper. On many companies' headed paper you will also see that the Unique Selling Proposition (USP) or slogan also appears.

Customers really couldn't care less about your logo. However, the CEO who was probably closely involved with the development and creation of the precious logo in the first place probably loves it most of all.

In tests it has been found that the best place to put your logo is *on the bottom* of your letter and *at the back (or last page)*. In this way, the first thing the recipient sees is a plain piece of paper. In fact, the logo is just another 'me' message. It says: *'Look at us, and look at our pretty logo.'*

Research shows that direct mail can work with *no logo at all* on your letter. Believe it or not in tests, blank paper gets a better response. I use it on occasion and I'm always happy with the results.

How important is your logo and corporate identity to your sales letter and envelope?

Answer: Not very. They usually reduce response.

Postcards

There is only one thing cheaper to send than a sales letter: a postcard.

Postcards work every time and can be powerful. Nevertheless, a postcard is not as successful as a sales letter. A letter provides a better chance to describe your deal properly.

You will recall that I said that the proposition would be the most important part of any mailing. This applies equally, and even more so, to postcards. Sometimes if your proposition or offer is straightforward enough you can simply print it artfully on the postcard and post it out. Sometimes the huge response you get from this is staggering.

Postcards are also good for promoting events, heralding the arrival of something new, reminding customers about the closing date of an offer or supporting a message delivered by a structured campaign of which the postcard might just be a small part.

But the best thing about sales letters and postcards is essentially that they are simply ink on ordinary paper. You don't need to add glossy brochures and full colour catalogues.

In my 25 years' experience in business and marketing, trying out many different things to see what works and what doesn't work for me, I have frequently been amazed to find that I get as good – or almost as good – a response from a simple sales letter, compared to sending the letter along with a glossy brochure.

There is even research to suggest that adding a brochure to a sales letter sometimes sends response *down*. Having a shiny A5 flyer fall out of the envelope can have the appearance of junk mail and immediately brands your letter as a mass mailing and a solicitation – for some recipients that means off to the bin it goes.

CHAPTER THIRTEEN
Constructive Criticism & Feedback

THIS SECTION INCLUDES:

- Everyone needs feedback
- How to receive feedback
- How to give feedback
- Feedback and sales copy writing

Everyone needs feedback

Wow! Now here's a topic that could probably sustain a whole book on its own.

In my view, feedback is probably the easiest, cheapest and most effective tool you can use to develop any task or project and even yourself.

Despite the massive potential and effectiveness of feedback it seems that it still remains a grossly underused tool – so just why is this?

Well I believe the sad and simple reason is that most of us are scared of criticism and often just can't handle it never mind welcome and encourage it!

I also believe that giving and receiving feedback is a skill like any other and as such it is one that we can work to improve if we really want to.

Feedback is fabulously useful in sales copy writing and I'll come to show you how you can use it for this shortly.

First, allow me please to share with you a few tips that will help you to give and receive feedback elegantly in all areas of your life.

How to receive feedback

1. Always ask people to give you feedback.
2. Tell them beforehand you don't care if it's flattering or not only that it's completely frank and honest.
3. Listen intently to the feedback and, whatever happens, if you hear something you don't like or disagree with don't go all defensive. The moment you go the slightest bit defensive in a feedback situation you have blown it. Most people are poor communicators so be sure to ask them questions and force them to be specific.
4. Remain impassive and emotionally calm throughout the process.
5. Thank them profusely for the valuable information and for their frankness. This way you will make it a lot easier the next time you want their honest feedback.
6. If the feedback was extensive, covering many items, than you should make some notes either during or immediately after the event.
7. Reflect on the feedback for a while after and determine what, if any, changes you will make in the future.

How to give feedback

1. Always start each session by giving at least one positive piece of feedback. Whenever possible, if you can't come up with something just say something along the lines of: *'I really liked the XYZ that you did.'*
2. Then say something along the lines of: *'And one of the things I thought you could do even better is . . . '*
3. Your goal should be not to activate defensiveness in the recipient. If you do you may end up encountering a strange kind of *defensiveness blindness* which may make your constructive message go unheeded.

Feedback & Sales Copy Writing

As I have said previously, I usually invite one or two people to read the first draft of my sales letter. They have to be people whose opinions I trust and whose feedback I value. However, if I involve too many people, I usually find their conflicting opinions tend to confuse more than they clarify.

A great method that serves me well is to gather all the feedback from my trusted *support team* but not make any changes until I've slept on it for a night. I frequently astonish myself with just how much copy I change for the better the next day. Feedback comments, that I was perhaps resistant to at the time, also get fresh consideration and I will often compromise a little even incorporating changes inspired by them. The end result? Much better copy than I would have had without the benefit of feedback.

If you are lucky enough to have any other accomplished writers in your advisory circle then you might like to invite them to shorten your copy without losing any of the persuasiveness. Occasionally you can get some real shocks here as people sometimes find new ways of saying what you said but in fewer words. Remember that when it comes to sales copy *less is more*. If you can say what you need to say in fewer words then usually you will find that those words have a whole new impact.

So feedback is a mighty powerful thing and if you are open to it you can use it to improve your life positively as well as your business and not just your sales copy. If you can use and embrace the feedback rules I've offered you above then I am confident you will see that they will have a monumental impact.

CHAPTER FOURTEEN
Measuring & Testing

THIS SECTION INCLUDES:
- Measuring
- Testing

Measuring

Measurement is crucial to success and has been mentioned repeatedly throughout this book. If you don't measure already you will know by now that you should start right now. Here is a list of a few of the most important things you should measure:

- The cost of each mailing
- The response
- The amount you convert to customers from response
- The profit on each initiative
- The residual sales of promoted products before and after promotion
- Labour: Don't forget to cost this in (even your own)
- Artwork and literature – these all have a cost too
- Returns due to any outrageous guarantees you make

The above are just a few of the things you can measure and there are many more. If you don't measure then you can't hope to run your business scientifically. How can you expect to run a business based on guesswork? If you rely on guesswork eventually you will come unstuck.

If you really are going to Test! Test! Test! You can't do this if you don't first: Measure! Measure! Measure!

Measuring isn't hard and it certainly isn't difficult, you just have to make sure you do it!

Sales letters are accountable

I did not invent most of the rules I'm sharing with you. They are fundamental to the practice of direct marketing in the real world, and have been derived scientifically by experts after years of testing and measuring.

Methodical testing provides valuable clues to what works, and what works brilliantly.

Testing

Some companies have mailing lists that run to millions of names. They take those millions and split them into two, three and maybe even four different segments. Sometimes these segments are divided according to a criterion such as age, or industry, or location. As I mentioned earlier, Tesco divide their lists into 30,000 different segments.

Each segment is tested by doing something different to the letter – for example, by adding or subtracting a PS – and analysing the results to detect whether the changed element has increased or reduced response.

This method is often called *A and B Testing.*

Test and then roll out

Imagine that you have several mailing lists, with four million names in total. One of the lists contains a million names. You could use the million-name list, and send out half a million letters with one headline. Then you could send the same letter, but with a different headline, to the other half a million. And then you measure the response.

Now you turn to the remaining three million – remember, half a million have received this letter already – and mail them the letter with the headline that you now know works best.

This is known as the *rollout.*

To my knowledge this kind of testing has been going on since about the 1920s, when the direct mail industry was born. Testing has been carried out for the best part of a century on countless millions of people.

Unfortunately, most of us don't have the luxury of owning huge mailing lists.

We all know the saying: *'The numbers never lie'*. If you can get your hands on enough statistics, you can see very clearly what is going on. However, it is much more difficult when you are in a small business, working with thousands of names rather than millions.

If we look at what happens when your customer base is relatively small it can be very difficult to test one headline against another, or to test a letter with no PS against one with a PS. But test them we do whenever we possibly can.

Afterword

You will doubtless recall my promise at the start of this book, which was to provide you with a simple guide for creating a sales letter. With this in mind, if I have in any way complicated this book then I will feel that I have done you a disservice.

However if you have just a little patience and you follow my instructions and advice I am sure you will create many, many successful letters of persuasion yourself that will win you many times the response you would have had, had you not decided to purchase this book.

You may also recall that I told you at the outset that it was never my intention to try and transform you into a Master Wordsmith. Perhaps I will undertake that challenge in a much larger book sometime in the future. In any case many excellent books by some wonderful authors already exist that will help you on your way to becoming an expert if that is what you really want. I have referred to many of these books as we've been going along and you will find details of them and other recommended books in the Resources Section at the back of this book.

In closing I feel compelled to add that your best teacher won't be me or any other author, lecturer or marketing guru. It will be experience and the actual application of my methods that will lead to your true mastery of them.

REPETITION IS THE MOTHER OF ALL SKILL

I would add to this my own quote:

"Expertise is forged in the crucible of trial and error."
– GARY COURTENAY

I want you to know that my methods work – not ALL the time but most of the time.

Please also know that I would not recommend to you or others anything that I have not personally tried and tested for myself. However, **don't take my word for it.**

I encourage you to go forth now and test my methods for yourself and if, for some reason, they don't work for you then please do let me know. Just to demonstrate my own passion and belief in that which I recommend and also my capacity to practice what I preach I remind you of my own personal guarantee:

my promise to you...

If you apply the principles, techniques and methods in this book and you fail to make many times more than the price you paid for it then simply return it to me for a rapid and immediate no quibble refund.

So confident and determined am I that you will enjoy either one or both of these benefits that should you, strangely, find this book does not deliver on its promise then I absolutely insist you return it for an instant no quibble refund plus your cost of postage. I have only one condition to this excellent offer. It is that you actually try out the ideas and suggestions first.

So go on, what are you waiting for? You hold in your hands the means to make several small fortunes or even one large one – the choice is yours.

I have shared many secrets with you in this book, secrets it has taken me a lifetime to learn and use. It has taken me 25 years to reach a level of competence where I can now share these secrets with you. But listen… come closer, for I have one last special secret to share with you. You see, I've been saving the best for last. *This secret is the most valuable one of all* for it really is the true secret of success…are you ready? Then here it is…

TAKE ACTION!

Go out with this information, use it to make money and use it to lose a little too and learn from this but just…

TAKE ACTION NOW!

Do it now, do it while you have the momentum of my inspiration behind you and my words in your mind.

MAY THE FORCE BE WITH YOU
(and the trend behind you)

Your friend in business

P.S. I respect your commitment in buying and reading this book and welcome your constructive feedback.

Gary Courtenay
Author, Speaker
and CEO of
www.mentors4business.com

Contact him at:
Tel: 08456 634 1400
Email: info@mentors4business.com

"All speech is vain and empty unless it be accompanied by action."
– DEMOSTHENES

FREE

£100 Voucher

**FOR A FREE EVALUATION OF YOUR OWN COMPANY'S SALES DOCUMENTS
BY
GARY COURTENAY**

All you have to do is send me your letter or advertisement, preferably by email as an attachment.

This voucher can also be used for any M4B product including consultancy, training, workshops, keynote speaches and software products. See the range available at www.mentors4business.com

Simply email your documents to Gary at info@mentors4business.com

Terms and Conditions

Vouchers are eligible for single use only. That means one voucher per book, per person or business. Please state your name and business, where you bought this book and the date you purchased it. No work will be carried out until this information has been given. Please allow approximately one month for return of work with feedback.

The offer is made in good faith and should not be seen as legally binding. The author reserves the right to withdraw it any time without prior notice.

Resources

Words That Sell
by Richard Bayan
This book is jam packed with useful words,
phrases and tried and tested headlines.
Published by CB Contemporary Books

How to Write Sales Letters That Sell
by Drayton Bird
In my opinion, after mine, this is the best British book on sales letters.
Published by Kogan Page

The Ultimate Sales Letter
by Dan S Kennedy
Dan is one of the world's best copywriters.
This book contains many nuggets.
Published by Adams media

Sales Letters That Sizzle
by Herschel Gordon Lewis
This book is a great source of gimmicks that work.
Published by NTC Business Books

The Tipping Point
by Malcolm Gladwell
An inspiring book about changing people's behaviour and 'stickiness'
Published by Abacus Books

The Pinnacle Principle:
How to Maximize Your Potential
By Peter Thomson
A recent offering from one of the UK's top business authors.
Published by Simon & Schuster Ltd. (UK)

Also from Peter Thomson: The Accelerated Business Growth System
Full details at: http://www.pti-abgs.com

Also from Peter Thomson: tgiMondays – Free Weekly Ezine
Full details at: http://www.tgimondays.com

Jay Abraham
http://www.abraham.com
Jay is most famous for his three day marketing seminars.
A full list of his books can be found on his website.

LifeTools
12 Tilbury Close
Caversham
READING
Berkshire
RG4 5JF
England

Tel: 01189 483444
www.lifetools.com
Chris Payne, the managing director is on
chris@lifetools.com

Appendix

Sample of letter referred to in the book

Providing *effective* nutritional supplements and exceptional service to health care professionals

30th August 2002

Mr AN Body
1 Any Lane
Any Town
Anywhere
AN1 WHR

Customer ID: 123456
Ask for Department: M0802

For the next month you can enjoy double the benefit of Nutri's best-selling caprylic acid formula on this great value promotion . . .

Dear Mr Body

NOW YOU CAN SHARE THE SECRET MANY ENLIGHTENED MEDICAL DOCTORS KEEP TO THEMSELVES

For the next month you can access **Exspore**, one of our most popular products, on a fabulous "buy one get one free" offer (worth £11.40 retail). **Exspore** is one of those rare supplements that frequently provides rapid results compared to the slower action of some natural products.

Exspore is also our most popular product with the medical doctors we supply, many of which buy **Exspore** in large quantities because they have found it to be an excellent alternative to certain prescriptive agents.

Amazing Powers

If you haven't tried **Exspore** yet then now is your chance to test it for yourself on these highly advantageous terms. If you are one of the thousands of customers that already appreciates **Exspore's** amazing powers then you will no doubt see this offer as a great opportunity to stock your shelves now, before the offer ends in just one month.

Buy 60 tablets of Exspore now and receive another pot of 60 tablets (worth £11.40 retail) absolutely free of charge!

This promotion is aimed at encouraging you to simply try this excellent product or to reward you if you have already discovered the many benefits of **Exspore**.

Please turn the page . . .

Cont'd . . .

The bane of western society

As healthcare practitioners, you are no doubt seeing an increasing number of patients whose health problems can somehow be traced back to poor gastrointestinal health. It appears to be the bane of western society, and many people are now paying a high price for a lifetime of inadequate nutrition and modern lifestyle habits.

Our health depends on a healthy balance of bacteria

Many different organisms live naturally in our intestines. More than 500 species of bacteria have been shown to inhabit the gastrointestinal tract, and about 30% by weight of human faecal material is composed of bacteria. Our health depends on a delicate balance between two main groups of micro-organisms, the "friendly" bacteria which are native to the gut, and the pathogenic bacteria.

Changes to the balance of bacteria can be caused by a variety of different factors, any of which can depress the immune system and kill off the friendly bacteria:

- Antibiotics
- Oral contraceptives
- Pregnancy
- Corticosteroids
- High sugar intake
- Life pressures
- Blood sugar imbalance
- Allergies

The stability of the gut flora may become severely disrupted

Potentially harmful organisms are normally kept in check by the friendly bacteria that colonise the gut. However, under certain circumstances, the stability of the gut flora can be severely disrupted, leading to an overgrowth of opportunistic micro-organisms. If these unfriendly organisms are allowed to flourish, they can cause serious gastrointestinal problems, and if left unchecked, may lead to chronic ill health.

Exspore helps support a healthy balance of gut bacteria

Supported by the most recent research, **Exspore** contains a synergistic combination of nutrients and friendly bacteria to help fight off opportunistic micro-organisms in the gut and support a healthy balance of gut flora. Included in this comprehensive formula are:

- **Caprylic acid**, a long chain fatty acid found naturally in coconut, which is well known for its gastrointestinal properties – and does not kill off the beneficial bacteria in the gut.
- Other botanicals such as **Garlic**, **Aloe Vera**, **Pau d'Arco**, **Tillandsia**, **Oregano Oil** and **Citrus Seed Extract**.
- 5 million units of the **beneficial bacteria** *Lactobacillus bulgaricus* and *Lactobacillus bifidus*.

As you've come to expect from Nutri, this all-round formula combines up-to-the-minute research with the best quality ingredients to ensure optimum assimilation and performance.

Please turn the page . . .

Sample of letter referred to in the book

Cont'd . . .

So why not take advantage of this fantastic offer and enjoy **double** the benefit, when you buy one **Exspore** and receive another completely **free-of-charge** during the next month.

Product Name	**Product Code**	**Pack Size**	**Trade Price (exc. vat)**	**Retail Price (inc. vat)**
Exspore	1532	60 Tabs	£6.50	£11.40

To place an order just call our friendly customer care team on **free**phone 0800 212 742 and **ask for department M0802**. This offer is valid until Friday 27th September 2002. Limited stocks have been allocated so call us now to take full advantage of this special promotion.

Yours sincerely

Katy Petter BSc (Hons)
Nutritionist

P.S. Avoid disappointment by ordering promptly. Take full advantage of this excellent opportunity for the next month and stock up now on **Exspore.** You will receive one pot of 60 caps (worth £11.40 retail) with every pot you buy **absolutely free of charge**! Stocks are limited so you should place your order now on **free**phone 0800 212 742 and ask for department **M0802**

"When it has to be *effective* . . .
it just has to be Nutri"

On this page is a letter written by Chris Payne, CEO at LifeTools.com, a UK-based mail order company, which was used to promote an audio course called PhotoReading. Notice the strong, powerful headline, which is designed to grab your attention and compel you to read the letter in full. If you would like a PhotoReading mailing pack to be sent to you so you can study it for tips on copywriting, email salescopy@lifetools.com or ring LifeTools on 01189 483444 and mention you heard about PhotoReading in Gary Courtenay's book.

Now! Revealed for the first time ever!...

The Astonishing Lightning Fast Reading Secrets Of A Painfully Slow Word-By-Word Reader

Learn How To 'PhotoRead' At 25,000 Words A Minute, Slashing Hours Off Your Reading Time And Tripling Your Comprehension

NEW! Learn to PhotoRead like a Pro by watching developer Paul Scheele demonstrate every step on video

Dear friend,

Let me ask you...

> Are you drowning under a flood of paperwork?
>
> Have you ever taken a briefcase home that's full of papers to read, then spent the evening pouring over them instead of relaxing?
>
> Did you know that, according to some research, people who read a lot earn two and a half times as much as those who do not? That means a salary of £50,000 instead of £20,000!

And would you love to be able to...

> Pass any exam with flying colours far more easily than you ever thought possible?
>
> Become an expert in any field in a fraction of the usual time?
>
> Get the important points out of any article in as little as two minutes?

If so, then read on!

Not so long ago I felt desperate. I had piles of books lying around unread and stacks of reports, magazines and articles.

I got so fed up to the back teeth that I learned to speed read, but I got only moderate results, and I quickly reverted to my usual bad habits.

Then I heard about PhotoReading. Supposedly you could learn how to blast through books at 25,000 words per minute – which was 120 times faster than my painfully

lifetools
230 Peppard Road,
Emmer Green, Reading,
Berks RG4 8UA
Tel: 01189 483444
Fax: 01189 482505

Chris Payne at LifeTools.com is a master at getting inspiring testimonials from his customers. This one is from his PhotoReading sales letter. When he finished the letter Chris showed it to a business friend who said: ‘Wow! This PhotoReading must be good if it’s endorsed by a university professor,’ so Chris put this particular one in a box to make it stand out.

your own pace in the least amount of time. By the end of the first tape you will be PhotoReading the dictionary included with the course, and having some amazing experiences.

What's more, PhotoReading does not require continual practice: once you've learnt the techniques you've learnt them for good...

...though of course it makes sense to PhotoRead regularly so you don't get rusty.

Just look what these people achieved!...

> "Best results: The feeling of having an overall understanding of a book after only 30 minutes using the PhotoReading Whole Mind System" – M King, Surbiton

"From scratch, I PhotoRead two months of Open University coursework and completed the associated assignment in one afternoon. I got 95% (I expected nearer 20%)." – I Doherty, West Drayton

> "Right at the start it helped me with my studying – made it more fun and it seemed easier." – Miss G Farrow, Walthamstow

"I read a book on Marxism for my Open University course and got 97% on the subsequent essay." – Mr Luka Rejec, Slovenia

> "Brushing up my Spanish with a BBC tape course, the new words and phrases seemed to leap out of the pages. Every prospective traveller should learn PhotoReading." – R Cunnington, Chelsea

University lecturer flabbergasted

"I PhotoRead and 'Activated' a new book on the Dead Sea Scrolls. It took me an hour and a half in total, then my wife asked me some quite detailed questions about it to check my level of comprehension.

"She was also very surprised to find that I could answer all the questions correctly. PhotoReading does wonders for the learning process.

"The techniques may be unconventional, but they certainly achieve remarkable results." – Dr George Chryssides, Senior Lecturer, University of Wolverhampton

"PhotoReading does wonders for learning," says Dr George Chryssides

Your questions answered...

What are the real benefits of PhotoReading?

You can get better grades at college, take up a part-time Open University degree and pass it with far less effort, improve your skills and contribution at work, and develop knowledge in other areas of interest to you at vast speeds.

You'll still be able to read at normal rates for pleasure reading, but your base reading rate will almost certainly double. Many PhotoReaders even PhotoRead a novel before they read it at normal speed because they say they get stronger imagery as a result, and they also get more engrossed in the book too.

Finally you'll be getting through every report, article and newspaper at incredible speeds, so you'll feel on top of your work, relieving you of stress and improving your sense of control.

Is it easy to learn PhotoReading?

Yes – anyone willing to learn can do it. I have taught the basics to an 8-year-old girl, and she was delighted when I proved to her how well she was doing. And we know of one PhotoReader aged 85! The innovative techniques really are straight forward and easy to put into practice. I got results within the first few hours of starting PhotoReading – and so will you.

Can I really learn to get through a book in 30 minutes?

Yes, really, over time. I was little more than a beginner at PhotoReading when I discovered I could do this

Here's a great set of bullets which Chris Payne at LifeTools used to promote the new Deluxe elements of PhotoReading to people who had bought the original PhotoReading audio course. He created the bullets by spending 3 hours watching the PhotoReading video and turning every solid piece of content into an exciting, attention-grabbing set of words to help sell the product.

Everything you need to get breathtaking results

The cornerstone of PhotoReading Turbocharger is the 50-minute video of Paul Scheele demonstrating all the steps of the PhotoReading system in front of four beginners. You'll discover...

- the fastest, smoothest way to turn pages at the rate of one a second or faster – see how to 'walk' your thumb and index finger
- exactly where you place an 'invisible tangerine' on the top back part of your head to open up your peripheral vision
- the science that explains why PhotoReading works so well
- the one key question to ask yourself after you've Previewed a book
- the 3 things you should have gained from Previewing
- 4 things you must do to get into an accelerative learning state
- 3 affirmations to say to yourself before you begin to PhotoRead
- the 3 crucial steps to getting into PhotoFocus
- the minimum time you must leave after you PhotoRead before you begin any activation
- the 4 important steps to take to activate any book
- a key question to ask before you even begin the Activation process
- a recommended maximum number of seconds to spend on any page while SuperReading
- why it's sometimes best to PhotoRead first before Previewing
- the benefits of PhotoReading a novel first before reading it at 'normal' speed
- the 2 beliefs you must have to ensure you succeed with PhotoReading
- the key similarities between how young children learn and how you PhotoRead
- 6 internal signals to watch out for which can tell you that PhotoReading is working
- 4 steps you can take to significantly improve your reading effectiveness even when you haven't done the PhotoReading step

... and so much more!

Sample of letter referred to in the book

Xandria Williams

M.Sc., D.I.C., B.Sc., A.R.C.S., N.D., D.B.M., M.R.N., NLP

Naturopath, Nutritionist, Herbalist, Homeopath, Reflexologist, Psychotherapist, NLP practitioner

Consultations:

London
e-mail: wzn@bigfoot.com

Correspondence:
Lower Sloane Street,
London
Ph/Fax 1234567890

Liver Detoxification: one huge step closer to better health

by Xandria Williams

Whilst studying to become a naturopath and nutritionist, I soon came to realise just how vital a perfectly working digestive system is to our health. I have since developed a particular enthusiasm for working with and correcting digestive problems, as it is commonly a first step to developing good health and well-being.

The next step, running a very close second, was to realise how important your liver is. It is a vital part of your digestive system, but it is also much more than that. It is, if you like, the receiving and processing plant that takes the food, delivered via your digestive tract, works it over, repackages it and then ships it out to the rest of your body for use.

The liver has literally hundreds of roles in the body

This may be for energy production, it may be for protein building. It may be repackaged fats so you can deliver cholesterol to nerve and brain cells, or rearranged amino acids so you have the specific ones you need. It may be iron in a form in which it can be delivered to the bone marrow for the formation of new red blood cells. In all these actions, and hundreds more like them, the role of your liver is vital.

Your liver is a pivotal player in dealing with toxins in the body

There is no system or part of your body that does not depend to some extent on the function of your liver or that may not be adversely affected if your liver is unhealthy, under-functioning or toxic. Your liver is an essential component, if not a pivotal player, in dealing with toxins in your body, either breaking them down into safer substances or eliminating them from your body, either as they are, or repackaged into a safer form. If all else fails, your liver will even store toxins itself, to protect the rest of your body. However, after a while, this act of generosity leads to liver damage and the rest of your body will suffer anyway.

Because of this amazing and central role that your liver plays, it becomes extremely important, in dealing with *any* health problem, to consider the state of your liver and the role it may be playing in both causing and trying to resolve the problem.

Failure of the liver to perform optimally can have profound results!

Just think what can happen if your liver fails to do its job properly. Because it plays such a vital role, it can affect the rest of the body in hundreds, if not thousands, of different ways. You could have indigestion, atherosclerosis, diabetes, hormone imbalances, PMS, period or menopausal problems or headaches and migraines.

You could develop allergies, leading to a vast range of symptoms ranging from eczema to asthma, from migraines to arthritis, from sinusitis to hives, behavioral problems, mood swings and mental confusion.

You could experience blood sugar imbalances with all the many associated problems, and hundreds of different vitamin and mineral deficiency signs. You would doubtless feel tired, for many different reasons, have poor skin and hair health. You could be an overweight but persistent yo-yo and unsuccessful dieter, and to cap it off your risk of cancer would be greatly increased.

Just think how many of your patients this list encompasses and that will give you some idea as to the huge number of them that might benefit from some liver support!

Detoxification problems – the silent cause

Detoxification problems may be the silent cause behind almost any symptom or health problem you may have. That's why it's important to undergo a regular detoxification programme, especially after periods of overindulgence, such as Christmas and the New Year.

Prevention is better than cure

Detoxification gives your liver a period in which it can "catch up" on itself, and get rid of all the nasties it has been storing around the body. This helps to leave you feeling cleansed, revived and thoroughly rejuvenated, not to mention helping to protect against future illness. It is, after all, much easier to prevent problems than to solve them and once you've convinced your patients of this they will be one huge step closer to better health.

The Book and the Product

As a result of my concern about and interest in the role of the liver I wrote **"The Liver Detox Plan"**. By the time I had finished that I realized that no reader was going to go out and buy, singly, each of the nutrients or herbs I had discussed as being needed by or useful for the liver. So I then put a formula together so that all, or most, of these things could be purchased in one product. Hence the **'Liver Support'** formula packaged in vegi-capsules.

Refusing to bow to 'market forces', I put in the expensive ingredients in the proportions I thought would be beneficial and the results have born out the wisdom of doing this. It has been a delight to me to receive, from both patients and other colleagues, the positive feedback on this product.

Yours sincerely,

Xandria Williams

Sample of letter referred to in the book

December 2002 • Ask for Dept M1102

Providing *effective* nutritional supplements
and exceptional service to health care professionals

NUTRI

Our previous Similase promotions have turned out to be a huge success - in fact they have been the most successful offers in the history of the company - and you will be pleased to discover that we are doing it all over again!

For the next 90 days, as part of this special repeat promotion, you and your patients have the opportunity to try Similase and receive an extra 20% free in an attractive, handy, pocket sized pack.

Dear Customer

Witness the powerful effect of Similase with your own eyes!

With Nutri, you always know you are getting the best quality supplements available. Because of the way most supplements work, it is not always easy to physically demonstrate their effectiveness. That is what makes Similase such an amazing product - it provides you with immediate, measurable results and a reaction that you can actually see. It is, quite simply, unique!

Benefits of a Plant-Based Enzyme Formula

- Aids the breakdown of proteins, carbohydrates, fats, fibre and sugars.
- Active across a wide range of pH conditions - from pH1 to pH12.
- By helping to break down food in the stomach for around 30-60 minutes or more before stomach contents are passed into the intestines, digestive enzymes help support the optimal absorption of nutrients from food.
- Helps to break down potentially antigenic constituents such as wheat and milk proteins.
- Maintains stability in the acid environment of the stomach, unlike animal derived pancreatic enzymes.
- Well-tolerated by sensitive individuals.

Developed following years of exhaustive research

Developed by Tyler Encapsulations of Oregon, USA, Similase has always been extremely popular with the thousands of complementary health care practitioners and their patients who order it on a regular basis, and has been their leading product for some time now. Similase was developed after years of exhaustive research by Tyler's own dedicated team of naturopaths and scientists, based on the very latest research into

Please turn the page . . .

Digestive problems - the scourge of the modern world

Due to numerous dietary and lifestyle factors, poor digestive function has become the scourge of the modern world, with more and more people suffering from a variety of gastrointestinal complaints.

Similase addresses the root cause of the problem, not just the symptoms

Unlike many other products that are supposed to support digestion, Similase has been designed to support the natural function of the body by providing the raw materials to help break down food properly, thereby supporting optimal absorption of nutrients and promoting gastrointestinal health. Clearly, for it to be Tyler's best selling product in the USA, Similase must be effective or practitioners and patients would not keep coming back for it time and time again.

But don't just take my word for it, witness the power of Similase for yourself and try this simple 2 minute test. . . Make up a small portion of porridge in a bowl. Stir in the contents of two capsules of Similase. Wait literally just a few seconds and what you will see is nothing short of amazing. As you stir, within seconds the glutinous mass of porridge will begin transforming into a light, watery liquid. The simple test takes just 2 minutes and very little effort, I cannot encourage you enough to try it for yourself.

If two capsules of Similase can transform a bowl of porridge and turn it into a watery liquid, then just imagine what it can do inside a troubled stomach to help break down its contents. And as you will see later, it works just as well under the acid conditions of the stomach!

So why take Similase?

As a health care professional, you will know the importance of proper digestion. It is a prerequisite for optimum health! Disordered or incomplete digestion can be a major contributor to the development of numerous health problems. Chronic digestive problems can lead to the development of sensitivities, as well as an imbalance of gut flora and the build up of toxins. These toxins may enter the systemic circulation, compromising health further.

Your job is set to become increasingly difficult

It is practitioners like yourself who understand these problems and have to deal with their consequence. There is of course no substitute for a good healthy diet, but unfortunately your job is set to become increasingly difficult as more and more people turn to poor quality, highly-processed, time-saving convenience foods.

How does Similase work?

In order for foods and nutrients to be assimilated by the body, they must first be broken down by enzymes in the digestive tract. Digestive enzymes taken as supplements during a meal can help to maximise the nutrient value of foods by supporting the breakdown process. This in turn helps to support optimal digestive health.

Similase is a plant enzyme formula which may help in optimising nutrient digestion by aiding the enzymes produced in the gastrointestinal (GI) tract to carry out their function more efficiently. It is important that a plant enzyme formula maintains stability in a wide range of pH, as the GI tract has a varying pH - from the acidity in the stomach through to the alkalinity in the small intestine. Similase contains enzymes which operate across a wide spectrum of pH values - from an acid pH of 1.0, through to an alkaline pH of 12.0. This provides balanced assistance for the digestion of protein, fats and carbohydrates.

The **Similase** formula also contains phytase which significantly improves the bioavailability of minerals by preventing their binding with the phytates in dietary fibre.

Enzymes are measured in units of activity. The Similase label clearly states the units of enzyme activity, not just the weight of the enzymes which gives no indication of their activity or efficacy. Most manufacturers do not put this information on their labels.

When should I take Similase?

Similase works best when taken just before a meal, although some people prefer to take it whilst already eating. Whether you are a very sensitive individual or you just have the occasional heavy meal, a digestive formula as gentle as Similase can be extremely reassuring.

Important Note: Similase is not intended for use by patients with gastric or duodenal ulcer, or with active gastritis.

Free handy pocket sized container

Because it is best to take Similase just before meals we are now supplying you, as part of this promotion, with a special convenient pocket sized pack that holds 18 capsules - handy for slipping into your purse or pocket, ready for just when you need them. You will be pleased to discover that we have enclosed one of these packs for your use completely **free** with this letter.

Receive 20% Extra Free with each 90 capsule size

We want you and your patients to try Similase because we believe that once you have experienced its unique benefits for yourself you will continue to use it. To tempt you we are giving you **20% extra free** for the next 90 days, when you purchase the 90 capsule size. The extra capsules will come to you in the same handy, pocket sized container as the **free** one enclosed. The cost of the 90 capsule size is £16.95 retail which is approximately one month's supply at the usual recommended dosage.

Please turn the page . . .

Sample of letter referred to in the book

If you have any queries regarding Similase then please call us now on ***freephone* 0800 212 742**, where the Nutri team will be more than happy to help you. To order just call us now on the same number and ***ask for department M1102*** and we will dispatch your Similase immediately.

Yours sincerely,

Sarah Gill, B.Sc.(Hons)
Nutrition Administrator

PS. When looking at supplements to add to our range, I am always looking for something a bit special, something that stands out from the rest - and when I first saw Similase I was truly impressed at the remarkable results. Similase is one of the few supplements I have ever come across that has an immediate effect and it really does work! I cannot encourage you enough to have fun conducting your own little experiment with Similase and porridge, and within seconds watch as the glutinous mass of porridge transforms into a light, watery liquid. I have found practitioners cannot praise Similase highly enough and I have enclosed just a few letters for your perusal from some of our many practitioners raving about the fantastic results they have had with Similase.

Regards,

Ken Eddie
Managing Director

Nutri Ltd,
Meridian House, Botany Business Park, Macclesfield Road,
Whaley Bridge, High Peak SK23 7DQ
Freephone 0800 212 742 · Freefax 0800 371 731

"When it has to be *effective* …
it just has to be Nutri"